**Praise for *Interrupti***

M000220845

"What are we missing about God, love, and life because of the ways we have constructed the modern categories of gender and sexuality? Without addressing this fundamental question, Christianity will continue to be stuck in colonial and capitalist frames of power where current heterosexism rooted. This book initiates a much-needed conversation."

—Joerg Rieger, Distinguished Professor of Theology, Cal Turner Chair in Wesleyan Studies, Vanderbilt University

"This is a fundamental book for those interested in the life of the Christian church as a place that honestly strives to live toward justice, equality, and honor. What we find here is a wealth of wisdom, powerful passion, and deep knowledge to build on an expanded notion of sexuality in relation to gender and race. Like the prophets who always interrupt us in our tracks, Anna Mercedes calls us to see, feel, change, and be transformed. Can we hear it?"

—Claudio Carvalhaes, associate professor of worship, Union Theological Seminary

# Dispatches: Turning Points in Theology and Global Crises

*Dispatches: Turning Points in Theology and Global Crises* draws on the legacy of early twentieth-century theological responses to the crises of the two world wars. During World War II, the Signposts series (Dacre Press, 1940) sought to offer an interruption of a theological malaise in the midst of mass violence and destruction. Contributors from that series, including Julian Casserley, Eric Mascall, and Donald MacKinnon, among others, offered slim volumes that drew from diverse resources and harnessed the apocalyptic political urgency of the dialectical school within the theological grammar of a more traditional Anglo-Catholic Thomism. Similarly, and inspired significantly by MacKinnon's contributions, this present series draws on diverse theological resources in order to offer urgent responses to contemporary crises.

While the title of the series conveys the digest nature of the volumes, the subtitle, Turning Points, indicates the apocalyptic urgency of the issues addressed, and yet reserves any prescriptive judgment on the manner in which the tradition can be reappropriated by our authors. In this way, we seek to offer a genuinely creative and disruptive theological-ethical *ressourcement* for church in the present moment. With conceptual agility and faithfulness, this series will provide intelligent and yet accessible reflections on the shape and form of theological life in the present.

Dispatches will illuminate and explore, creatively and concisely, the implications and relevance of theology for the global crises of late modernity. Our authors have been invited to introduce succinct and provocative arguments intended to provoke dialogue and exchange of ideas while setting in relief the implications of theology for political and moral life.

## Series Editors

Ashley John Moyse (PhD, Newcastle) is the McDonald Postdoctoral Fellow in Christian Ethics and Public Life, Christ Church, University of Oxford. In addition to his work with the Dispatches series, he is the author of *Reading Karl Barth, Interrupting Moral Technique, Transforming Biomedical Ethics* (Palgrave, 2015) and *The Art of Living for the Technological Age* (Fortress 2021). He has also coedited several volumes, including *Correlating Sobornost: Conversations between Karl Barth and the Russian Orthodox Tradition* (Fortress, 2016), *Kenotic Ecclesiology: Select Writings of Donald M. MacKinnon* (Fortress, 2016), and *Treating the Body in Medicine and Religion: Jewish, Christian, and Islamic Perspectives* (Routledge, 2019).

Scott A. Kirkland (PhD, Newcastle) is the John and Jeane Stockdale Lecturer in Practical Theology and Ethics and research coordinator for the Trinity College Theological School, University of Divinity, Melbourne. He is the author of *Into the Far Country: Karl Barth and the Modern Subject* (Fortress, 2016); coauthor, with John C. McDowell, of *Eschatology* (Eerdmans, 2018); and coeditor, with Ashley John Moyse and John C. McDowell, of *Correlating Sobornost: Conversations between Karl Barth and the Russian Orthodox Tradition* (Fortress, 2016) and *Kenotic Ecclesiology: Select Writings of Donald M. MacKinnon* (Fortress, 2016).

## Published Titles

*The End Is Not Yet* by John W. de Gruchy
*Political Orthodoxies* by Cyril Hovorun
*Theology and the Globalized Present* by John C. McDowell
*Theology, Comedy, Politics* by Marcus Pound
*The Art of Living for a Technological Age* by Ashley John Moyse
*Interrupting a Gendered, Violent Church* by Anna Mercedes

## Forthcoming Titles

*Theology in the Capitalocene* by Joerg Rieger

Interrupting a Gendered,
Violent Church

# Interrupting a Gendered, Violent Church

Anna Mercedes

Fortress Press
*Minneapolis*

INTERRUPTING A GENDERED, VIOLENT CHURCH

Cover image: *Yes. Surrender. Bloom.* (Number 2), Ashon Crawley, 2020, mixed media
Cover design: Kristin Miller

Print ISBN: 978-1-5064-3159-8
eBook ISBN: 978-1-5064-5834-2

For my children, Sylva, Norah, and Clare,
in honor of the worlds they will shape

# Contents

*Acknowledgments*                                            xi

*Preface*                                                    xv

1.  Complicit Church                                          1

2.  Circulating Christomodern Power                          49

3.  Assemble Otherwise                                       99

*Afterword*                                                 155

*Selected Bibliography*                                     165

# Acknowledgments

I thank my faculty and staff colleagues and my students at the College of Saint Benedict / Saint John's University for providing me with a Benedictine home base for this work. I thank my theology faculty colleagues for their feedback on a portion of this book's argument at our winter 2020 Pursuit of Wisdom gathering. I feel particularly accountable to my students, past and present, as I write: thank you for your passion, your questions, and your affirmation—let's keep going together.

I thank my colleagues at the Upper Midwest Regional Meeting of the American Academy of Religion in April 2021 for their responses to a portion of my argument.

I thank Luther Crest Bible camp in Alexandria, Minnesota, for hosting an annual women's week. It's nothing short of a miracle what you do: creating a space for a mother to be with her children and be fed while her kids are busy with fun and inspiration, so that this mother is able to live out her vocation and write theology. There were two years running when that one week at camp was my primary writing time for the year. I pray for more communities for more parents.

From the initial sketching of the project on through the years to a very different final product, I am very appreciative for the supportive collegiality of series editor Ashley John

Moyse. Ashley's steady confidence and enthusiasm kept me committed to the writing vocation when so much else tried to block my momentum. I am also grateful to series editor Scott Kirkland for his constructive suggestions on the text and to Will Bergkamp at Fortress Press and Elvis Ramirez at Scribe Inc. for shepherding this book along its way to publication!

I thank my former teacher Traci C. West for encouraging me to keep putting pen to paper when my momentum and confidence were lagging. I thank Ashon Crawley for allowing his art to coalesce on the cover with these words.

I thank three particular groups of people for helping me to know the textures of the improvisational abolition about which I write theologically here: my practice partners and teachers in somatics for social change; my dance partners in contact improv; and the community in constant vigil at George Floyd Square at Thirty-Eighth Street and Chicago Avenue in Minneapolis. You texture the otherwise that inspires me; you welcome new incarnation.

This book benefited greatly from draft readers who gifted me with feedback on all or part of the manuscript: Brandy Daniels, Kayko Driedger Hesslein, Stephanie Hart, Linda Noonan, Autumn Brown, Laura Taylor, Anna Blaedel, Cláudio Carvalhaes, Robyn Henderson-Espinoza, Anja Woulu, Quinn Brakob, and Sylva Mercedes Bohannon. Writing can be lonely; thank you deeply for making it less so.

Through her own professional career, my mom, Susan "Bruce" Nolan, has always been proof that a strong woman can interrupt when something needs interrupting. And on top of that role modeling, Mom is also the one who delivers groceries and goodies so I can stay in and keep writing. Thank you, Mom!

I am especially grateful to the network of friends and chosen kin that support me. Though this network is wide and varied, I am attached to each of you in your particularity. You know the ways. Thank you for what we share between us and what we have become together.

I dedicate this book to my children. The bulk of this work was written during a global pandemic when they were at home and isolated from peers. I thank them for their own improvisations in navigating life with a mom/writer, mom/teacher, and mom/priest, especially during a time that was particularly turbulent for our family.

Sylva, Norah, and Clare: To have at first cradled you, and now to be yielding to you, and—when invited—to bear witness to *your* world-shaping is a prismatic, sparkling gift you give me, just by being your *you*. Your worlds, which need not match one another's and need not match mine, shall be my joy.

# Preface

For this series of books on contemporary crises and church response, I set out to write a dispatch on how church people could think about the modern controversies around gender and sexuality. I planned to offer a kind of tour as a teacher of theology and of gender studies. I would explore some of the trickiest topics and point toward some of the liberative ways churches might approach them.

I soon realized I couldn't proceed honestly with this approach. I'd been deeply influenced by J. Kameron Carter's *Race: A Theological Account*, and through Carter, I'd come to see how Christians were funders of the modern racist project in which they are now so deeply entangled. With Carter's work in mind, I looked at the map I was ready to tour, particularly at all the sites labeled "sexuality," and came to a stop. I realized I couldn't take church people on a tour without the advisory warning that their churches were primary cartographers of the map itself, as seen in a faded signature smudged away at the edge of our map—a map that has now become a scientific diagram, legitimized and sanctified by both church and science.

In this book, I take a magnifying glass to that signature. Imani Perry writes in *Vexy Thing*, "We can say, and it would be true, that the accumulation of gender domination falls more heavily on some shoulders than others. That can be an assertion. But we must also attend to how that happens. The deeper charge is to move beyond assertion and, through careful examination and shifting maps of attention and relations of care, toward a transformation in how we exist in relation to others so we might transform our analytical practices, and with growing facility, witness the unjust processes of accumulation, deprivation, and depletion so that we are able to disrupt domination."[1]

My goal in this dispatch is to bring that kind of examination and disruption to the churches, specifically through attending to Christian complicity in the construction of the concept of "sexuality" in the modern West. I will explore sexuality as a thing thoroughly comingled with the concepts of race and gender, all three rooting in modern Christian colonialism. Shortly put, I argue that the churches, whether progressive or conservative, are too often oiling the modern machine of "racialized, ableist heterocapital"—a phrase I echo from Alexis Pauline Gumbs.[2]

When I first heard that precise phrase from Gumbs in the forward to *Beyond Survival*, the church-sponsored machine I'd been scrutinizing for this book finally had a name: "racialized, ableist heterocapital." My church, your steeples are mortared by it. Take them down. Assemble differently. This dispatch is a call to Christians to divest from the colonial

---

1   Imani Perry, *Vexy Thing: On Gender and Liberation* (Durham, NC: Duke University Press, 2018), 249.

2   Alexis Pauline Gumbs, foreword to *Beyond Survival: Strategies and Stories from the Transformative Justice Movement*, ed. Ejeris Dixon and Leah Lakshmi Piepzna-Samarasinha (Chico, CA: AK, 2020), 2.

mechanics of sexuality, which is to say, a call to queer and darken Christian practice.

Before I continue, I want to offer clarity on how I am using *sexuality* here. The word *sexuality* is used in many ways, often distinguished from gender or sex or even "having sex." In this book, by *sexuality* I mean that category of desire or attraction that has come to be understood as somehow internal to a person as an essential structure of personality and identity. A person might describe their sexuality with various names: gay, straight, asexual, bisexual, and "homosexual" are a few.

While distinct from them, the concept of sexuality is bound together with the categories of *gender* (a social category organizing social roles, for example, "woman") and *sex* (at the same time a problematically biological category that organizes bodies—for example, one's assigned sex at birth—and also a shorthand word for some categories of "sexual" activity, as in *having sex*). These concepts are all knotted together.

In this project, the key concept under scrutiny is the idea of sexuality construed as an essentialized inner category fundamental to personhood. As such, that sexuality is closely connected to another concept—*sexual identity*—and the very idea that we would have such an identity is again tied to sexuality as an internal category of personhood. Knots.

The main argument of this book is that Christian churches need to raise their awareness of their tradition's role in implementing the concept of sexuality as an essentialized inner category of desire integral to selfhood. Sexuality is a modern project considerably structured and funded by Christianity. As such, most all contemporary Christian responses to sexuality, be they liberal or fundamentalist or anything else, start in medias res. We may think we are trying to come to the scene of a modern controversy and faithfully respond as Christians, but in fact, our tradition and its institutions have set the scene. Yet many church people often ignore, or are unaware of, any Christian complicity in this "sexing" project that harms and controls. Even those that do acknowledge this harm often don't regard Christians as original authors so much as current contributors. Thus this dispatch focuses on stressing the churches' role in producing and then also maintaining modern regimes of sexuality.

I also offer here a sketch of theological possibilities divested from this regime. When the churches recognize their role in bodily colonization, the recognition demands action, because church institutions capable of such a role are revealed as dangerous and violent. If in theological teaching and in practice churches have been machines for the mechanics of producing sexuality in modernity, a shared understanding of this history and complicity can help people of the churches live their faith differently for the sake of our bodies and lives—which is also to say for the sake of ongoing divine incarnation in our world.

How might we assemble differently, improvising sacrament and embodying nonviolent ecclesiologies? I bring the gender theorist in me to my work as a theologian and pastor as a way of helping articulate the future that might be possible for Christian practice after so much of what we have known to be church falls away as we divest of the colonial mechanics that have now become nearly indistinguishable from Christianity.

# 1

## Complicit Church

In her book *Shameless*, Nadia Bolz-Weber candidly and compassionately explores the difficulties of navigating sex amid all of Christianity's obsessions with it. As a pastor, she wants more thriving for all people and a more widely shared recognition that God's love is not bound by sexual rules.[1]

In his book *Dear Church*, Lenny Duncan lovingly calls out the church's interwoven white supremacy, sexism, and heterosexism. He helps the church imagine a future that is "gloriously queer" and also makes it clear how painfully far the church has been from celebrating such a future.[2]

Bolz-Weber, Duncan, and I have all served as pastors and are of similar age; in our lifetimes, there has never been a time when the churches in the United States were not wrapped up in some kind of issue related to sexuality—both the most "conservative" and the most "progressive" groups

---

1   Nadia Bolz-Weber, *Shameless: A Sexual Reformation* (New York: Convergent, 2019).
2   Lenny Duncan, *Dear Church: A Love Letter from a Black Preacher to the Whitest Denomination in the U.S.* (Minneapolis: Fortress, 2019), 79.

of churches. A church full of discourse on sex has been the church of our times.

Thus it is no surprise that many people in and out of the churches wonder why Christianity seems so hung up on sex. We notice that Christian organizations seem both fixated on sexual teaching and at the same time entangled in sexual misconduct, abuse, and scandal. We notice that, on the individual level, many Christians will speak of or even define their faithfulness predominately in terms of their sexual ethics or choices. As Mark D. Jordan insightfully notes, "People who know nothing of Christian creeds or scriptures can recite the most notorious Christian sexual prohibitions. . . . In the public imagination, Christianity can figure as nothing more than a code of sexual conduct, a code that likes especially to elaborate prohibitions."[3]

These fixations on the institutional and individual levels are far from coincidental, because Christian discourse and polity are so deeply embedded in the modern mechanisms of sexuality. The mechanisms are now so subtle and efficient that we have arrived at a time in the modern West when you can barely do one without the other. One certainly cannot tell the story of modern sexuality without exposing the Christian underpinnings. Whether one can tell the story of Christianity without becoming entangled in the regime of modern sexuality is an open question. This writing is driven by the hope that Christian practice can in fact flow free of the mechanical workings of "sexuality" that have corrupted its energies for so long.

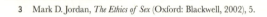

---

3  Mark D. Jordan, *The Ethics of Sex* (Oxford: Blackwell, 2002), 5.

Thus—though you might pick up a book by this title because you want to think more about what Christians teach about particular sexual issues or decisions, or how the church can respond to gender-based violence—this book will not speak directly to those questions. It sits a conceptual step before them. It seeks instead to highlight ways in which every Christian stance on sex and gender is already an iteration of a larger Christian project in forming the gendered and sexualized lives we live and the issues for which we now seek a stance. If we Christians have positions on these issues, they are stances on our own products; they are therefore our own self-critique, though we seldom acknowledge them as such, preferring instead to blame an elusive secular or popular culture. And it is odd and sly, and also dangerous and even immoral, of us Christians to promulgate juridical teachings for individuals concerning a fraught situation we have in the first place underwritten. It is as though we, who as Christian agents helped create the hazardous playing field, now give instructions for how individuals should play on it, and we are ready with shaming and punishing measures for those who don't play nice and conform. We enforce personal labor for what is actually a public project and in so doing manage to veil the publicness of the construction and make it "private" business. Thus the work of our Christian cultural production is carried out by individuals, bodily carriers who take the blame and bear the brunt and punishing weight, meanwhile shielding the insulated systems that shape the whole domineering project. Often, as individuals, we shield those systems even from our own consciousness and punish ourselves, shaming and abusing our own bodies and those of others.

These are heavy claims with which to start a brief book. I will explain these claims more fully as we go; for now, notice that the fixation of churches on "sexuality" is an important "tell" revealing the success of what I will call *Christomodern* power strategies. That we are fixated on sexuality and busy maintaining it as a category—busy embodying this category and thus *incarnating* the power it serves—Demonstrates how thoroughly we as Christians have bought into this way of organizing and controlling bodies.

## Three Moments

Here is the story of three moments that helped me realized the needfulness of this dispatch on the Christian production of "sexuality" and the ongoing Christian enforcement of its terms.

### 2006 View Im 2006

The large, active congregation in which I was raised in the southeastern United States asked me to come and speak to them on the occasion of their centennial. A PhD student at the time, I ambitiously decided to speak on "One Hundred Years in Theology." I am sure now that I couldn't have possibly lived up to that title in an hour, but I did aim to include major movements of the twentieth century in US theology, including the beginnings of gay and lesbian liberation theologies. I remember that during the Q&A, a longtime member, Doris, asked a generous question about supporting LGBTQIA life, and in answering her, I surprised myself by saying that it wasn't enough to raise questions of queer theology out of concern for gay and lesbian lives—though that concern is vital. I knew the congregation to include supportive people concerned about queer lives and loves, and I remain grateful to have grown up in that church. But it came out in my response that day that it wasn't enough to just be concerned about an inclusive response to queer individuals in church or society. There was a bigger conceptual problem at stake that affects the church's life as a whole.

Analyzing heterosexism in the churches and in theology shouldn't only be about needed concern for the well-being of LGBTQIA persons; it should also be about recognizing the severe brace that such heterosexism has placed on our cognitions and our theological imaginations. What are the churches, or what is theology, consistently missing about God and about love, about human life as a whole, because of the strictures of heterosexism? So I told my childhood church that we need to critique heterosexism not only out of our commitment to social justice—though our world needs that desperately—but also out of our thirst for God, our desire to walk humbly with God, which can perhaps surprisingly appear as determination to scrutinize whether our cultural worldview, or our popular or working philosophy, has limited our vision of and our life with God. I argue that heterosexism, and the whole structure of sexuality on which it rests, has indeed done so. The church is chasing the tail of its own constructions while the world aches for what the churches could instead be offering.

What does the Bible teach?

5

## Ten Years Later

Around midnight, as it was becoming clear that Trump would win the White House in 2016, I was huddled in a dim bedroom trying to settle one of my young daughters back down to sleep. As she dozed back off, I was scouring the *New York Times* on my phone in the dark of her bedroom, looking for articles that helped me understand Trump's victory. In "A Pennsylvania Town in Decline and Despair Looks to Donald Trump," Trip Gabriel tells the story of a town that was once strongly aligned with the Democrats but was now firmly for Trump in this election.[4] Gabriel introduces the Cranos, a couple that had been pulling for Hillary Clinton in 2008. Now the couple was voting for Trump. What changed their position? Gabriel reports, "For Mr. Crano, a former steelworker who retired after a second career at the Pittsburgh airport, it was abortion and same sex marriage. 'If you're a Christian, you can only vote for Trump.'"

In the quiet of a night, reading this article on my phone as I tried to figure out what sort of America I would wake up to the next morning, this statement of Crano's stunned me. I can understand a sentence beginning with "if you're a Christian" ending in something like "you can only follow Jesus" or "you must worship Christ." Things like that. But to be a Christian equals . . . a particular sexual position? How had being Christian become completely aligned with particular views on sexual issues? What had become of my religion?

---

4    Trip Gabriel, "A Pennsylvania Town in Decline and Despair Looks to Donald Trump," *New York Times*, November 9, 2016.

And what happens when such a stance—standing with particular political leadership because of a "Christian" stance on sexuality—means utterly failing at other aspects of the Christian life, such as hospitality to the vulnerable, as in the Bible's injunction to care for the "widow, the orphan, the stranger"? Or ignoring the more tacitly accepted political angles of our sexual politics, like misogyny, sexual misconduct, and the abuse of women? When did we, Christians, become agents of sexual patrol and allow ourselves to ignore the wider work of our faith?

Because at the time of that election, my gender theory students were reading Mark D. Jordan's *The Ethics of Sex* and thus scrutinizing with Jordan how our Christian rhetoric on sex raises as many or more ethical problems as our sex lives themselves, I heard in Crano's remark proof that a commitment to a particular sexual ethic can indeed involve a major ethical breech in Christian life. Our religion has conspired in creating a rhetoric on which we now fixate and with which we distract ourselves to great peril from the lives Christians could be living in service to God's world. In defending particular positions within our logics of sex, we are defending not the God of the Scriptures but, plainly, our logics of sex. No Christian statement on sexuality can be adequate if it does not recognize Christianity's role in shaping what we know as "sexuality." Such shaping is our largest sexual "sin"—the major issue behind all other Christian sexual "issues."

## Third Moment

A group of college faculty from multiple disciplines was discussing white racism in conjunction with a campus grant on improving learning outcomes for students of color in the United States. The discussion turned to what the institutions could do to declare their commitments to countering racism. I teach at Catholic and Benedictine schools, and noting our mission, colleagues wondered whether our Catholic, Benedictine values on hospitality and dignity of all persons already gave us our way of expressing an institutional commitment to counter racism. Other local state-funded schools have more explicit antiracism programs. For us, some wondered, does a reassertion of our Benedictine values "cover it"?

As one of the theologians in the room, I felt an urgent need to speak an emphatic "no." Lest anyone assume that being Christian already puts in you in a stance against social oppression, I felt compelled to emphasize that Christianity is at the root of many social oppressions in the first place. To point, one cannot invoke Christianity to counter racism without recognizing that Christianity is largely responsible for creating the concept of "race," or said differently, that race is a Christian theological by-product. Far from being a mode of liberation from racism, Christianity is built into the beams of modern racist structures. I directed my colleagues to the work of Carter in his *Race: A Theological Account*. And I became involved in directing our next inclusion grant.

It was later, working on that next grant project and having been asked by colleagues to address how to reconcile our Catholic identity with support for trans students, that

I started to argue that the same can be said for Christian responses to sexism and heterosexism. To the extent that the modern logics of sexuality are Christian theological productions, Christians cannot adequately engage their corruptions without isolating Christianity's ongoing production of the "sexuality" with which we can do modern "sexism" and "heterosexism." To put it harshly, we can't declare ourselves inclusive, even with wide-open arms, when there is structural blood on our hands.

## Connecting Fields and Conversations

In the fields of gender and sexuality studies, it is not a contentious claim but rather a familiar one that what we now know as "sexuality" in the West is a modern and recent thing.[5] There is general agreement that "sexuality" developed conceptually very recently, has a great deal of power clustered around it, and was a discourse of power to begin with. Inarguably, we have had human bodies and contact between human bodies, some of it erogenous and some of it reproductive, for all of human history; that is different from the modern category of sexuality. That is all much less specific than what we now file in the conceptual category of

---

5    H. G. Cocks and Matt Houlbrook, *The Modern History of Sexuality* (Hampshire, UK: Palgrave Macmillan, 2006). To explore the history of sexuality as a modern concept, this book by Cocks and Houlbrook is a great place to start, as is Veronique Mottier, *Sexuality: A Very Short Introduction*. (Oxford: Oxford University Press, 2008). I also direct the reader to Anne Fausto-Sterling, *Sexing the Body: Gender Politics and the Construction of Sexuality* (New York: Basic Books, 2000); and Christopher Chitty, *Sexual Hegemony: Statecraft, Sodomy, and Capital in the Rise of the World System* (Durham, NC: Duke University Press, 2020).

"sexuality," even if we now think of sexuality as a wide category rooted in the core of each human.

I write on this topic influenced by teaching in theology and being a pastor. The histories of how modern sexuality came to be understood have begun to seem obvious to me after years of simultaneously teaching gender studies courses alongside my theology courses. But I have become increasingly aware of a gulf between what was seemingly obvious to me and what the givens about sexuality are for many of my theological colleagues. Certainly, in pastoral work with churchgoers, I still encounter a sense that gender and sex just are—as givens, not social products—or at best I encounter the idea that sex and gender are societal or secular topics to which responsible churches will respond. But it's more surprising to me to encounter this sense in the academic and clerical theological guilds. Yet I still do, where colleagues who teach, preach, or write on sex do so from a place of big heart and willingness to work on important topics but where the conversation still proceeds as though sex and gender are cultural products out there for us to engage theologically rather than largely theological products for which we were always already particularly responsible as Christian theologians.

When I think of sex and gender as such, I find that I come to conversations about them from a different theological angle, and that is one I would like to share more widely with colleagues in the academy and in the churches. Thinking as I do of modern sex and gender as largely theological cultural products, I respond to questions of theological ethics around them a little like I might to questions about a house I designed if I learned that it now had leaky pipes. Rather than only coming in to patch the leaks, I would also be thinking about what in the design led to leaks, I would be willing to scrutinize and share my blueprints if that might help the people living in the house fix the situation, and perhaps most importantly, I would be willing to take responsibility and to work toward restoration and repair.

To follow this analogy, what I too often encounter in Christian discourse on sex and gender—even when full of good intentions—is conversation on the leaks, the damage done by the leaks, or the lamentable situation of our neigh-bors with the leaks and how we should help them dry up and find a better place. This all seems a little hypocritical to me when I think about how we helped build the house. Someone should be pointing their finger at us. In doing so here in this text, I also intend for Christian people to step up, repent, and repair, yet with a sense of greater transparency and respon-sibility for our role in the production of the hazardous con-structs of sex and gender in contemporary society.

Thus, with this dispatch, I hope to make the standard point within gender studies of sexuality's relative novelty more familiar in Christian academic and congregational contexts. The second goal of the book is to emphasize the church's role in this modern mechanism of sexuality. While it is hard to deny that Christianity was a major shaper of the modern West, there is not yet widely shared attention on how much that shaping was specifically sexual, on how much the churches have been a sexing stamp on modern culture. From there, it is just a short step to the third goal of this book: to argue that Christians can respond differently to the contemporary crises around sexuality when they recognize their tradition's original and ongoing shaping power in the situation. Christians can position themselves differently in regard to "sexuality." Divesting of Christomodern violence, Christians shift into the coalitional practices of the emergent holy. Unbound from the Christomodern economy, Christians sink more deeply into the work of the gospel in birthing power differently and diffusely in the world.

Christians can divest of coloniality's strategies. They need not offer another set of speeches on sex or a list of new rules. That would be another "power over" move, another supersession, which would only continue the sexing machine. Instead, Christians can divest of coloniality and invest in nonmodern collaborations: flowing with them, serving them, and where possible, vivifying them.

Simply, the first goal stands on its own as constructive for contemporary church people. Once I came to assume as a matter of course that sexuality is a modern construct, it changed the way I thought and taught Christian history and the Bible, and it changed my approach to contemporary Christian ethics and theology. My second goal is the heart of the matter for me, because therein lies our complicity and responsibility as Christian people. And the third goal is a hope for you, a hope that you will take up this work of different responsibility with me in plural ways wherever you are now.

## But Surely Sexuality Is Ancient?
## Exploring the "Before" of Sexuality

At some point in this reading, as has happened repeatedly when I try to make this argument in conversation, you may find your mind backing up. Such as, "But wait, gender is really old; I know ancient civilizations had men and women." Or, "Wait, heterosexuality is ancient; I mean, procreation relies on it and clearly that has been happening for a while?" It makes sense to think these things; after all, gender and sexuality are primary categories of *how we think* at all in the late modern West.

But while people have undoubtedly been making babies through history, and we have any number of artistic artifacts that show the proof of long-standing eroticism, "sexuality" as we know it is newer. And while we see ways of marking sex difference in bodies and social roles—differences related to that bodily diversity—"gender" as we know it is also newer. And importantly, both are specific to a colonial frame of power.

"Sexuality" and "gender" as concepts blend into each other and are inseparably enmeshed with the concept of race and the mode of colonization. Thus, when you are speculating "behind" or before early modern colonization (or into the "noncolonial" that exists today[6]), you can find many cognate concepts for ways humans categorized life and organized social power, but they had different ways of conceptualizing and different social intents. Inevitably, we

---

6   María Lugones, "Toward a Decolonial Feminism," *Hypatia* 25, no. 4 (2010): 742–59.

read backward with some of the bias of our current categories, so we can never know the full intent of the older
words and concepts. But we can at least remind ourselves
that our own concepts are not timeless and ubiquitous, even
if—especially if—they seek to shore up a power that intends
to be so. This is also true for trying to understand not only
the past but also differences across contemporary cultures
now. A two-gendered binary system of heterocapital is *not*
the only option currently embodied on the globe or even in
places marked by Western dominance; it *is* a standardizing
feature of late modern Western hegemony.

María Lugones makes it clear that "gender" can't be
thought of in separation from race, sexuality, or the colonial. As DiPietro, McWeeny, and Roshanravan explain,
"The hallmarks of Lugones's theory of gender are, first, that
it recognizes the differential ways that gender is constructed
in relation to Europeans/whites and colonized/nonwhite
peoples, and second, that it sees the concept of gender as
a colonial/modern imposition developed in the service of
consolidating and facilitating the global exercise of power
in Eurocentered capitalism."[7] Lugones's phrase "colonial/
modern gender system" emphasizes the contextuality of
those things we easily think of as ancient, whether gender,
race, or sexuality. Living under the colonial/modern gender system, what we often think of as gender is part of a
binary, not of man and woman, but of light and dark. The

---

7   Pedro DiPietro, Jennifer McWeeny, and Shireen Roshanravan, eds., "Like an Earth-
    quake to the Soul: Experiencing the Visionary Philosophy of María Lugones," in *Speak-
    ing Face to Face: The Visionary Philosophy of María Lugones* (Albany: State University of New
    York Press, 2019), 16.

more familiar binary of man and woman is only a subpolarity within the "light" side of the system. Heterosexuality is therefore also on that light side. And the "dark" side functions to uphold and legitimize that light side. That is, dark "others," colonized "others," function as ungendered bodies, like animals, not quite human. In contrast, the gendered are the light men and women, in heterosexual pairing, and that pairing is a snapshot of colonial capital. It is a still frame for "racialized, ableist heterocapital," the phrase I have been using from Alexis Pauline Gumbs.

Considering the idea, perhaps for the first time, that sexuality is not a timeless given but a product of Christian colonial hegemony can feel befuddling. Even those who are confident about the devastating ills of Christian colonialism in slavery and genocide often still hold onto the inner category of sexuality, even if they leave Christianity itself behind as part of their decolonial path. It's as though sexuality is some quaint and benign remnant of the old owner's style in our house, a remnant we simply forgot to remove. But far from harmless, the inner concept of sexuality is a mechanism of the controlled construction of our bodies at the level of reproduction itself and our relationship to our most "private" desires and experiences: at the level of how we live as bodies, feel our pleasures, share or constrict our bodies, and conceptualize the age and worth and ability of our bodies. As such, the tenacious concept of "sexuality" lingers more like unchecked lead poisoning than a harmless remnant.

When my theological students are becoming accustomed to the idea of sexuality as a recent construct, a frequent question is, Hasn't the church always taught about sex? (After all, for many young adults raised in churches, church has mostly been a set of teachings about sex.) They also raise similar questions such as, Doesn't the Bible have a lot to say about sexuality? What did Jesus teach about sexuality? Didn't the church fathers have a great many church "rules" about sexuality? (Someone with a lot of church school in their background will often bring up Augustine here!) Or, after I've stubbornly insisted that homosexuality is not in the Bible, we come to question, But surely there is *heterosexuality* in the Bible?

These are great questions as we try to think ourselves out of a hegemonic hold on our minds and bodies. Nonetheless, this word "sexuality," so far as it denotes a personality's innate category of desire, had no foothold before modernity. Thus, to try to answer these queries about "before," we need words that applied before "sexuality." For example, we can talk about bodies and pleasures (I borrow those from Mark Jordan, himself inspired by Foucault), or we can talk about eroticism. Trying for something like "reproductive acts" or "genital acts" is (boring and) too narrow for the things we might be asking when we wonder about how some of what we pack into the concept of "sexuality" might have been present for humans in earlier periods.

The story of Christianity and erotics and bodily pleasure is its own tale, a plural tale, richly worth exploring.[8]

---

8   See Margaret Kamitsuka, ed., *The Embrace of Eros: Bodies, Desires, and Sexuality in Christianity* (Minneapolis: Fortress, 2010); Peter Brown, *The Body and Society: Men, Women, and Sexual Renunciation in Early Christianity* (New York: Columbia University Press, 1988); Virginia Burrus, *The Sex Lives of Saints: An Erotics of Ancient Hagiography* (Philadelphia: University of Pennsylvania Press, 2003); Virginia Burrus, Mark D. Jordan, and Karmen MacKendrick, *Seducing Augustine: Bodies, Desires, Confessions* (New York: Fordham University

Consider with me three short examples that help emphasize the continuities and shifts between these contexts and the modern regime we now know as sexuality in the West.

## Example One: The Bible and Queerness

First, a biblical example. We know that the Bible was written in ancient languages, as Greek and Hebrew are still spoken today but now in different, modern forms. But there is less recognition that the concepts of the Bible were also ancient, and where something like the concepts still persist today, there are now very different forms. We read something in the Bible about use of the body for pleasure, usually male pleasure, or the use of the body for reproduction, and we think: sexuality. We read something about men with other men, and we think: homosexuality. But in doing this, we are translating the Bible with modern vernacular that doesn't accurately apply to the biblical context. We could easily be missing the original speaker's message because we're listening through our own filters. In other words, we could be missing the Bible's point and using it to make our own points instead. A classic example of this is the way in which Genesis 18's glaring message about hospitality to the divine in

---

Press, 2010); Rosemary Radford Ruether, *Christianity and the Making of the Modern Family* (Boston: Beacon, 2000); Virginia Burrus and Catherine Keller, eds., *Toward a Theology of Eros: Transfiguring Passion at the Limits of Discipline* (New York: Fordham University Press, 2006); *Sexuality and the Sacred*, in both significantly different editions (James B. Nelson and Sandra Longfellow, eds. [1994], and Marvin M. Ellison and Kelly Brown Douglas, eds. [2010]); Kathleen Talvacchia, Mark Larrimore, and Michael F. Pettinger, eds., *Queer Christianities: Lived Religion in Transgressive Forms* (New York: New York University Press, 2014); and Merry Wiesner-Hanks, *Christianity and Sexuality in the Early Modern World: Regulating Desire, Reforming Practice*, 3rd ed. (London: Routledge, 2020).

our midst, even in our midst as a stranger, can be thoroughly lost through reading the story as one about "sexuality."

Misreading of the Bible is a familiar accusation thrown at people like me who are theologically and politically liberal, but it is an equally valid risk for people who are theologically and politically conservative. It is a risk for anyone most familiar with and comfortable with their own cultural vernacular, which is to say, it is a risk for nearly everyone. Learning about how norms for what we now call sex and gender were different in the various biblical contexts from what they are today is a step toward mitigating our own contemporary bias when we read the Bible.

In his *God's Beauty Parlor*, Stephen Moore offers a reading of Romans 1 that highlights the erotics of social power driving Paul's portrayal of idolatry in that letter. The inversions of the idolaters in Romans 1 are emblematic of idolatry, demoting the Creator beneath creatures, because they are inversions of social hierarchy. The erotics that matters for interpreting Romans 1 is not a modern homosexuality read backward onto the passage but rather a (disturbing) erotics of social power in which God is always on top. Here God is The Top, and God's virility is proven by divine penetration of all those who play the bottom to God.[9]

An internal, essentialized sense of sexuality does not help interpret the theology of idolatry that Paul presents; such a thing is foreign to his context, an anachronistic concept.

---

9   Stephen Moore, *God's Beauty Parlor: And Other Queer Spaces in and around the Bible* (Stanford, CA: Stanford University Press, 2001).

Instead, Paul resonates with his context in understanding a social order based on hierarchically organized bodies. His was a context of a one-sex system in which bodies had one perfected form, solid and virile, epitomized by the erect phallus (right down to common household decorations shaped as such).[10] Divinity then reflects that form, and since idolaters put God on the bottom, they, in this logic of Romans 1, get their orders of penetration all mixed up. They worship the creature as the Creator, they put women on top, "idolatrously" imagining that a fluid body lacking virility can penetrate and thus dominate. They flip the order of things in that worldview.

Moore's reading of Romans 1 opens up a clear example of how our best analysis of the erotics of a time can help us understand what is going on with bodies in a text and how that relates to the theology given by the Bible, while meanwhile our contemporary lens of "sexuality" can profoundly skew the theological message available in the Bible. As Moore summarizes after having examined the sex-gender system operative in Paul's context, Paul's theology, "traditionally thought to be encapsulated in his letter to the Romans, was not only *infected* by this sex-gender system put partly *produced* by it." Reading bodies and pleasures in the Bible as we code them nowadays will not open up the theologies of its authors, while trying to understand the uses of bodies operative in a cultural system or a biblical

---

10   An image of such an ancient wind chime, and a discussion of the "one-sex" and phallus-focused culture from which it comes, is found in Mottier, *Sexuality*, 8.

text gives us inspiration and room for nonmodern readings, theological strategies, and embodiments today.

## Example Two: Early Church and Marriage

Often older contexts can surprise us when we let them. One strong example is the early church contestation of marriage, which is so different from prevailing Christian understandings of marriage in the United States today. As Mark D. Jordan writes, "Especially when it comes to sex, Christianity is a discourse that enacts supersession while forbidding return. The patriarchs were commanded to be polygamists. . . . But no Christian may be a polygamist. Indeed, it has been a disputed question whether Christians should marry even once."[11]

Dale Martin's article on "Familiar Idolatry and the Christian Case against Marriage" shows how different early Christian norms were from the hegemonic American "family values" of today. Martin elaborates many examples of ways that "the vast majority of the resources of scripture and Christian tradition until the modern period lend themselves much more readily to a critique of marriage and the family than to advocacy of them."[12] From Jesus asking "Who is my mother and who are my siblings?" to Luke and Acts and the book of Revelation presenting "Christian community as displacing marriage and family and replacing

---

11  Mark D. Jordan, "The Return of Religion during the Reign of Sexuality," in *Feminism, Sexuality, and the Return of Religion*, ed. Linda Martín Alcoff and John D. Caputo (Bloomington: Indiana University Press, 2011), 48.

12  Dale B. Martin, "Familiar Idolatry and the Christian Case against Marriage," in *Sexuality and the Sacred: Sources for Theological Reflection*, 2nd ed., ed. Marvin M. Ellison and Kelly Brown Douglas (Louisville, KY: Westminster John Knox, 2010), 430.

them with new eschatological social formations,"[13] Martin shows how very different Christian teaching on marriage was before modernity, which is also to say, before "sexuality." Martin details how in the late fourth century, for example, Jovinian was excommunicated for daring to teach that marriage might be equal in value to celibacy (rather than celibacy being the clear winner!). Overall, Martin offers Christians resources to critique what he terms "the modern idolatry of marriage and family."[14] In our exploration here, that idolatry can be understood as part of the outworking of "biopower"—a concept to which I'll return later.

As another example, sometimes a contemporary artifact related to the body and sex stands as full opposite in function to a similar artifact in an ancient context. The power of Thecla's celibacy in the Acts of Paul and Thecla establishes a counter patriarchal power, her own authority. She renounces the marriage her father has chosen. She becomes not a servant of Paul but, inspired by Paul, an established spiritual source for others. And her celibacy is part of that power.

The contrast of Thecla's story with that of a young woman at a contemporary "purity ball" in the United States is striking. Jessica Valenti's *Purity Myth* explores the disempowering dynamics of teaching young women to find their worth in their sexuality and their chastity.[15] In the case of purity balls, a girl's father is often seen as the protector of

---

13   Martin, "Familiar Idolatry," 420.
14   Martin, 431.
15   Jessica Valenti, *The Purity Myth: How America's Obsession with Virginity Is Hurting Young Women* (New York: Seal, 2019).

her chastity until she is given to a husband. The heteropatriarchy here hardly needs elaboration (and it is in fact not a medieval story but a contemporary American one!).

Whereas for Thecla, chastity resists—in the name of Christ—the patriarchal control of her day, for the girl at a purity ball, her chastity marks her taught deference to the Christian patriarchal control of her day. In one instance, "purity" stands as resistance to patriarchy; in the other, purity stands as capitulation to a patriarch, as the capital of patriarchy.[16]

Adding another layer of contrast, a study like Anna Adams's "Perception Matters: Pentecostal Latinas in Allentown, Pennsylvania," can show that for some contemporary women in the United States, chaste sexual choices can be a mark of empowerment, an exertion of bodily choice in a racist cultural context that tries to take that autonomy away.[17] This is a strong contrast to the purity ball example, where choice and power remain in the domain of the (often white) father.

These examples, whether ancient Thecla or present-day Allentown, show varied economies of bodies and social power and show how hegemonic power makes more difference than bodily acts in determining how a body's pleasures are codified. Uses of bodies and pleasure, even the same uses or acts in different contexts, mean vastly different things

---

16  On these dynamics in Thecla and others of the same period, see Virginia Burrus, *Chastity as Autonomy: Women in the Stories of the Apocryphal Acts* (Lewiston, NY: Edwin Mellen, 1987).

17  Anna Adams, "Perception Matters: Pentecostal Latinas in Allentown, Pennsylvania," in *Reader in Latina Feminist Theology: Religion and Justice*, ed. María Pilar Aquino, Daisy L. Machado, and Jeanette Rodríguez (Austin: University of Texas Press, 2002), 98–113.

when read in terms of the social power at play. Accordingly, the contrast between female celibacy as protest of patriarchy in some contexts and female celibacy as allegiance to it in hegemonic white US Christian culture brings a hermeneutics of suspicion to just what might be implicated in that hegemony. From this vantage, for those wanting to deconstruct white Christian hegemony, the often-critiqued hookup culture does not seem as dangerous as the more insidious hitch-up culture. Christian efforts to critique hookups can then function as hidden endorsements of the hitch and the white Christian power it protects.

## Example Three: Reformers and Monastics

Another story of bodies in varied relation to Christian power structures can be seen in the Reformation's impact on monasteries. Luther's movement worked to decentralize Christian political power in the West, and for some of what would become the Protestant traditions, his movement also worked against the idea that individual action, including any "sexual" ethics, would matter for salvation. But at the same time, the Reformation worked to support the cementing of the institution that we would eventually know as the heterosexual family. And it literally closed down the alternative to patriarchal family units that monasteries could sometimes serve as.[18]

Luther's own celebration of the man-and-wife family helped name physical intimacy as a sacred good in the context

---

18  Merry Wiesner-Hanks, ed., *Convents Confront the Reformation: Catholic and Protestant Nuns in Germany* (Milwaukee: Marquette University Press, 1996).

of monastic celibate ideals, but as Roman Catholicism then clamped down at the Council of Trent on clerical celibacy—after ample evidence of leniency on the issue—in juxtaposition to the renegade marrying Protestants, the Reformation thus helped further a dichotomous insistence on celibate male clerics on the one hand and man-woman intimacy on the other. Though the political heterogeneity and the lessened hierarchal potency of the Reformation offer the possibility for decentralized messaging about church teaching, including that around what the modern age would term *sexuality*, the Reformation's idealizing of man-and-woman marriage as part of their political strategy of dissidence would serve a later purpose at odds with the original strategy.

One cannot know the mind of the Reformers, and as people of their own historical period, they would no doubt be befuddled by much in our time, but the way in which their movement balked at Christian policing of morality in economic repercussion and moral shaming seems to indicate that the way Christian discourse on sex functions today would remind the Reformers much more of the imperial Christianity they sought to resist than the reformed Christianity they sought to establish. It is at least ironic that their work in part helped create the later imperial Christian messaging around the goods of the family, which would come to carry an intense disciplinary function.[19]

\* \* \*

---

19  A good resource to further explore the topic of Christian formation of the modern family is Rosemary Radford Ruether, *Christianity and the Making of the Modern Family*.

These scattered examples show tiny snapshots of the much larger story of how the connections between bodies and social power have shifted dramatically through the history of Christianity. In modernity, we arrive at a cultural power structure in which bodies themselves become the territory of coloniality, which can therefore function as geographically borderless. Bodies come to have an inner territory, "sexuality," which can quietly be leased or farmed out to the regime such that it can seem as though you are making personal or faithful choices with a particular part of your life rather than handing over your body, your "self," to a system of control.

Thus, despite the ways one might trace an absence of Christian power in modernity—a lack of religiosity as the mark of modernity itself, such that Christendom is often seen as the thing left behind by modernity—scrutinizing the sometimes hidden operations of Christian power in our bodily lives instead reveals a significant, ongoing, subterranean Christian force in modernity. Yet still for many, Christianity has seemed the thing lost by modernity, not its parent and ongoing funder, making the disciplinary functions of Christian power even harder to recognize around us.

Accordingly, for many, the discourses of sexuality in modernity, as an age of sexual liberation or an age too sexually libertine, have seemed to be clear markers that separate this era from Christendom. That is not the case. Sexuality (always bound together with race and gender) is a modern child of and an *ongoing project* of Christianity, though other significant forces (scientific, governmental, capitalist) also carry the project now.

Well-intentioned Christian people unknowingly contribute to the ongoing Christian production and reinforcement of sexuality in ways that then cause concrete bodily harm. Christians thus need to do more than speak up about sexual justice as they define it, whether "conservative" or "liberal." They need to interrupt their own speech about sex, their own thought about sex, in order to break their theological body habits and rededicate themselves to whatever other theological practices and habits await their attention when they are no longer misdirecting their energies into the project of modern "sexuality," which is at once none of their business (as a misdirection for the energies of the mystery of God in the world) and largely their business (as a discourse with manifold physical ramifications for which they share responsibility).

What can seem like simply a topic within contemporary Christian theology (sexual issues or sexual ethics) is actually a primary way of analyzing the way Christian power operates in the modern West. That is, the analysis of sexuality and Christianity—inseparable from race and Christianity, or gender and Christianity—is a way toward assessing and perhaps redirecting Christian political theology, not on a particular subtopic, but overall, in the churches' relation to modern power regimes.

## Essentialism and Social Power

The concept of gender essentialism helps me express the ways in which Christianity has shaped the seemingly essential artifact of internalized, individualized "sexuality."

Gender essentialism shows up when people talk about there "being" certain genders that just, simply and fundamentally, are. Essentialism presents things as how things always were. (To hold up, this claim must ignore or negate the plentiful contemporary and historical anthropological and cultural differences in concepts like gender.)

Judith Butler's work most precisely helps me explore with students a key danger of gender essentialism: the way it masks the creators of "essence."[20] In occluding the social shapers of "essence," gender essentialism presents as a given our gendered beings and thus forestalls any questions about how things came to be as they are. They just are, essentially, as a given. Perhaps even a God given!

In contrast, a constructivist argument turns our scrutiny instead to the projectors of any essences or identities. The point of a constructivist approach is not simply that culture and society shape who we are (though that's commonly where people stop in their query of it, simplifying it to "we're all culturally constructed, nurture over nature!"). Rather, the point of a constructivist approach is that in order to reshape power relations in culture and society, we don't simply notice that things are constructed rather than essential but instead ask of the constructions, Why? And for whose benefit? Analyzing social construction not only sets people loose from a sense that they "should" be a certain

---

20    See Judith Butler's *Undoing Gender* (New York: Routledge, 2004) or her seminal *Gender Trouble* (New York: Routledge, 1990). For theological discussion of the topic, see Joseph Sverker, *Human Being and Vulnerability: Beyond Constructivism and Essentialism in Judith Butler, Steven Pinker, and Colin Gunton* (Stuttgart: Ibidem-Verlag, 2020); and Serene Jones, *Feminist Theory and Christian Theology: Cartographies of Grace* (Minneapolis: Fortress, 2000).

way (which is already a liberative effect of theory) but trains them into the habit of asking, What is this cultural machine doing, who set it up, and why? Who benefits from the construction of this apparent essence?

These questions need asking for the supposed "essence" of sexuality in the modern West. Once we ask these questions of sexuality's "essence," it begins to seem clear how nonsensical and potentially dangerous it is for Christians to enter the discourse seeking to construct a sexual ethic or response to issues of sexuality as though they are issues presented to us by the present age or by contemporary culture. To do so is to arrive so deeply enmeshed in medias res, so deeply in the middle, that we too easily forget there was an entrance at all and just understand the thing to be how things are, to be the given of human embodied life. It seems like everyone just naturally *has* a sexuality—whether we defend it or try to repress it in the name of God.

Therefore, every tenet we teach about sexuality ("speeches," as Jordan calls them in *The Ethics of Sex*),[21] whether in clarifying the straight and narrow or expanding the welcome of the churches, is playing its part in the script of sexuality already set out for us by Christian production. Under these conditions, "conservative" and "liberal" sexual teachings end up serving the same endgame of furthering the Christian project of bodily control in modernity.

In the meantime, divergent teachings do continue to effect real and very different lived conditions for Christian persons, and those effects matter profoundly, so this is

---

21    Jordan, *Ethics of Sex*. See, for example, 5, 138, or 172.

not to say that various teachings are equally harmful but rather that they are all likely serving the ongoing effectiveness of the discursive setting of sexuality as a violent concept among us. They continually reify the certainty that "sexuality is a thing, and I can have one," as David Halperin has so aptly summarized the tidy packaging of this modern concept.[22]

Accordingly, in his *The Ethics of Sex*, Jordan does not so much write—as the title might suggest—an ethics of what might be moral, or not, in all things sexual. Rather, he queries more primarily the ethics of Christian discourse on sex in the first place. Jordan notes that while Christians may want to blame the surrounding culture for their fixations on sex, "we Christians would do better not to excuse ourselves so quickly" and instead "might want to consider our bad habits, our vices, when it comes to setting forth a Christian ethics of sex."[23] In this text, Jordan scrutinizes not particular ethical stances but the doing of the sexual ethics at all. Is the Christian enterprise of sexual ethicizing itself ethical?

Jordan urges his reader that "responding to ideological discourse requires a rule, not just of suspicion, but of inversion: we should attend not to what the discourse says, but to how it operates."[24] Jordan takes up this task with Christian sexual ethics and shows how Christian speeches on sex serve to bolster Christianity as a system of domination

---

22  David M. Halperin, editor's introduction to *Before Sexuality: The Construction of Erotic Experience in the Ancient Greek World*, ed. David M. Halperin, John J. Winkler, and Froma I. Zeitlin (Princeton, NJ: Princeton University Press, 1990), 5.

23  Jordan, *Ethics of Sex*, 5.

24  Jordan, 151.

and control—not just in content but in form and function.[25] In contrast, Jordan inspires new theologizing as he gestures toward what might be left for Christian aspiration around bodies and pleasure when we interrupt the noise of Christendom's speeches on sex.

It was in reading Jordan's *The Ethics of Sex* that I first began to reshape my ideas of what was wrong with "sexual ethics" in my church (and Jordan's subsequent writing guides the entire argument of this dispatch). Jordan's argument about the rather unethical way that the discipline of Christian sexual ethics functions *to discipline*, in a uniquely modern insidious fashion, fully changed my approach to helping the church.

Since my days of youth group leadership in my teens, and as the daughter of a skilled mediator, I'd wanted to speak up for healthy conflict processes in churches and how they could be transformative. I thought that being able to talk openly and with good facilitation about our stories surrounding sexuality and our disagreements about sex would be the healing the churches needed. I had big dreams for my church back then, and I am still a fan of openness and good facilitation! But the enduring nature of church fights about sexuality have seemed particularly tenacious and intractable as the years have passed. And reading Jordan with my students, I finally started to refocus my gaze, not on Christian arguments about immorality in any one particular sex life, but instead, prior to any such determinations, on the

---

25  Jordan writes in *Ethics of Sex* that "theologians no longer speak as officers of Christendom; they ought not to speak as delegates of bio-power"—yet "too many church speeches will want to do one or the other" (138).

"sexing" power mechanics supported by Christian arguments on sex.

When I later encountered J. Kameron Carter's exacting argument that the modern concept of race has a theological character that the conceptual framing itself seeks to mask, his work pushed me to recognize a similar furtive and insidious masking in the framing of sexuality.[26] Both "race" and "sexuality" are framed with a kind of dissolving frame—that is, both are concepts designed to mask their own status as concepts and to instead appear as givens. Borderless, uncreated, essential, as though they are not cultural constructs, not ideas set up this way: they simply are this way. All persons simply have a race and a sexuality, right?

Following this false but common logic, the ethics are in what we do with race and sex, not in making the conceptual boxes that got us here! That widespread essentialism around sexuality and race is a trick Jordan and Carter helped me recognize as such.

Keeping up this trick of masked racing and sexing of the contemporary body corrodes the heart of the church. The trick kills, making consistent violence against others, and frequently against the self, seem justifiable or even necessary on the basis of supposed essential qualities. Behind the trick is the reality that these individually experienced qualities have been classified and weighted by someone else. Someone benefits. Thus the classifications and weights we often experience as "ours" when it comes to what we think of "our" race and sexuality are actually "theirs"—those

---

26    J. Kameron Carter, *Race: A Theological Account* (Oxford: Oxford University Press, 2008).

institutions and individuals who helped construct the categories we later come into as our "self"-realization. As I'll explore in the next chapter, María Lugones's work helped me make further connections between race, sexuality, and gender; these three come into focus in the same frame when one looks through the lenses of church and colonialism at the same time.

The argument of this dispatch will seem absurd so long as we think of sexuality as an innate component of human personality. For if it is that, how can it be produced? How can it be a production of religious political systems and power plays, as I explore here?

And yet—as creatures of our time and place, bodies formed in current conditions of power—so many of us experience sexuality as precisely this fiction: as a part of who we are and how we understand ourselves, a key step in our coming of age, part of an existential programming. We don't stop to ask, Programming by whom? We assume DNA, or God.

It is nonetheless possible for us to think differently without losing our agency and pleasure (we can perhaps even gain in these). Your body's pleasures and potencies, boundaries and comforts, urges and wants, connectivities and satisfactions can still be valid and real—can even be potent fuel for how you navigate the world—without being conceptualized as an inborn essential programming chip, as though imagined underneath your belly button somewhere. We can imagine instead other bodily topographies and corridors for the sexual: more mobile, transitory, malleable and less fixed, essential, frozen.

We can reimagine the sexual as patterns and powers by which we connect and disconnect. As a language with which our bodies write and speak. As one of our mediums for world making.

That which we experience as "sexuality" does not have to be innate—does not have to be "sexuality" at all—in order to be sacred.

Not all of social construction is malevolent; part of it is the fabric of our richly social subjectivity. As Judith Butler writes, "On the one hand, everyone is dependent on social relations and enduring infrastructure in order to maintain a livable life, so there is no getting rid of that dependency. On the other hand, that dependency, though not the same as a condition of subjugation, can easily become one."[27] And under the mechanics of racialized, ableist heterocapital, the construction of "sexuality" does effect a malevolent grid upon which we come into "our" selves, to the brutal extent that only some lives are even valued as worthy of grief and some lives bear too much of the weight of the social grid to be survivable at all.

Christian colonial hegemony persists in this tricky enterprise to the point of a hardening of the heart that is nearly fatal for the churches. In contrast, when church people recognize the dangerous mechanics of racing and sexing that their Christian institutions, teachings, and practices are supporting and divest, we encounter a fresh pulse for what

---

27   Judith Butler, *Notes toward a Performative Theory of Assembly* (Cambridge, MA: Harvard University Press, 2015), 21.

the heart of Christian practice might be. The churches are already irreparably damaged; there is no clean start for Christian practice after such a bulky history of colonial (pre)occupation. We divest not with any sure confidence for what will be left of the church but with heightened clarity that what we have been doing in regard to race, sexuality, and gender has in fact not been "church" after all. We've tricked our own selves into a false belief of what Christian ecclesial embodiment must be. We go forward not with confidence for what we can save of the church but with curiosity and desire for our Christ's ever-new, messy body birth, which was always supposed to be our passion anyway.

## Querying Power, Queering Power

With groups, I like to introduce feminist theories of power with an exercise I call "power play." I ask the group to volunteer all the words that jump to mind when they first hear the word "power." A trend emerges, time and time again. Words emerge such as *leader, control, government, CEO. Authority, law management, boss. Domination* or *dominion* (both of which share the root for the English word "Lord"), *might, rule, sovereign.*

We generate many words, but a theme underlying many of the initial words that arise is a sense that we are talking about power *over* something or someone. In other words, often when people in my contexts think of power, they immediately think a kind of top-down, coercive force. This impression runs so deep that for many people, "power" could simply be restated as "over," as a kind of "overness." To be over equals having power.

On deeper inquiry, we can readily recognize more forms of power, like the way we use the word to mean electricity, as in when "the power was out." We also use it to mean ability: "Does the crowd have the power to sway the governor?" And in the sense of physical science, we use it to mean ability for movement ("The tow truck has enough power to haul my van.") So: energy, force, brawn, ability, momentum. These uses of power emerge as people brainstorm too, sometimes even as the first illustrations, but I have never yet had them emerge in the group activity with as much dominance as the idea of power as dominating!

Then there are notions of power I sometimes have to supply for the group. If they haven't arisen spontaneously, I add to the board power as generation, capacity, birthing, influence, facilitation, fostering, even a personal favorite, lactation. Overall, I try to help the group identify both our tendency to equate power with dominance and our ability (our power!) to claim other forms of power that are nondominative. I sometimes name these other modes of power *generative power* or *creative power*, so long as the group explores how those phrases are slippery because dominative power can also manufacture or produce.

The real challenge in my "power play" activity involves the next step, when I ask small groups to embody nondominative or generative power together, ideally without words (think charades). They get time to work on this as a small group; then they come back together and show the rest of us how nondominative power might take form in our bodies together.

As Lisa Isherwood has aptly observed, power is "an issue that feminists have had more ease denouncing than claiming."[28] When it has explored claiming power, feminist theology has celebrated—in contrast to "power over"—notions of "power with" or power together. Feminists generate power in shared and collaborative forms. I think for example of Carter Heyward's "theology of mutual relation."[29] Or, I treasure Rita Nakashima Brock's portrayal of "Christa/community" in her "Christology of erotic power." Brock writes that "we are called not to dependence on a power outside ourselves, but to an exploration of the depths of our most inner, personal selves as a root of our connections to all others."[30] And elsewhere I have joined the feminist theological discussion of power by nudging us past power with and articulating Christology as a domain of "power for."[31]

For the sake of the present inquiry, I have briefly described "power over" and powers otherwise in order to help approach the concept of biopower as we think about the power at play in "sexuality" and church. Indeed, I join Brock in calling us away from dependence on any dominating

28 Lisa Isherwood, "The Embodiment of Feminist Liberation Theology: The Spiraling of Incarnation," *Feminist Theology* 12, no. 2 (2004): 140–56, this quotation 143.

29 Carter Heyward, *The Redemption of God: A Theology of Mutual Relation* (Lanham, MD: University Press of America, 1982).

30 Rita Nakashima Brock, *Journeys by Heart: A Christology of Erotic Power* (New York: Crossroad, 1988).

31 Anna Mercedes, "Christ as Chrism, Christ Given Away," *Dialog: A Journal of Theology* 53, no. 3 (2014); and Mercedes, *Power For: Feminism and Christ's Self-Giving* (London: T&T Clark, 2011).

power "outside ourselves," but the concept of biopower helps me name how deeply "power over" can get under our skin. Power over can begin to move through us, to saturate and contaminate our categories for the erotic, for pleasure, for creativity, for comfort, and for our sense of self. As biopower, dominating power keys directly into that sense of self, even and especially that self's "biology." Those categories for the erotic, pleasure, creativity, and comfort come to be largely tucked away behind the concealing walls of your "self" or your body, an enclosure that at least constrains and at worst fully blocks the coalitional character of these things.

As biopower, "power over" has gotten under our skin, where the "inner" and the "personal" function as intense sites for social control that are too easily hidden. Power over functions effectively under our skin, not only in teaching us dominative postures, but most poignantly in teaching us to enforce those postures on ourselves, teaching us to discipline ourselves on behalf of another's terms, while thinking it personal work. As biopower, power over adapted, went underground, and dissembled as power *through* our own selves.

## Cellular Power

Building from the modes of power discussed in the previous section, we can think of biopower as belonging to the power-over category while being so insidious that it becomes a kind of "power over/through." This internalized embedding of power, throughout and within individual bodies, disguises it and occludes it from easy analysis. As such, biopower is powerful in a frightening and yet intimately familiar way.

Biopower is a concept developed by Michel Foucault and one applied by many theological authors, with Mark D. Jordan and J. Kameron Carter being two crucial theological interlocutors of Foucault for the present volume. Biopower is a way of naming a furtive, domineering, social-engineering force that operates within a people or culture rather than overtly over them—as with a king or obvious sovereign—but nonetheless controls them. Biopower is possibly even more successful than a discrete sovereign power in getting the people to own hegemonic ideas and actions on their *own* as interior to them. Think for instance of "your" sexuality: what could be more personal or interior than that? (Perhaps, disturbingly, your faith or spirituality?)

Yet who taught us to think of sexuality that way? Who benefits? What *don't* we see while we are distracted by the supposed freedom of managing or "discovering" our sexuality? Its efficacy is in its ability to mask the "over" feel of this power, giving us a seeming ownership of it. What we perceive is not power over/through but only a power through us. Thus we can feel, depending on our positions in the overall social economy, strong and capable. Self-work and self-definition can feel like our power in contradistinction to dominating social power, not its continued iteration. Power through can feel like power through *me* to make me free. But it remains power over/through; it is power *over and through me* to make my "freedom" function within established constraints. I can more easily stomach this kind of power over than an old-fashioned dictator (it is as internally familiar as my stomach!). As Cocks and Houlbrook write, "Modern Western societies, Foucault suggests, require us to

govern ourselves, to be 'free' within certain limits, and the 'invention of sexuality' has been a key technique of getting people to do this."[32]

There are many beneficiaries of modern biopower, from big pharma to the fashion industry to various patriarchies in households and in workplaces. But the emphasis of this book is that Christian powers continue to benefit, that Christian hegemony and dominance (which are also white Christian supremacy) are served by the interiorized conceptual placement of "sexuality" and by the ways we are then programmed to manage and maintain it, doing the production work of "Christian" culture along the way while we instead supposedly think ourselves to be doing personal work, finding ourselves, coming out or coming into ourselves, and measuring our worth, our appeal, or our morality in terms of "our" sexuality. But "sexuality," along with race, is a major operation manual of modern Western culture inlaid within us, programmed to look individualized, to appear deeply intimate and look like it is "ours," such that listening to these inner drives feels personal but is also adherence to the steps it takes on a corporate level for us to continue promulgating Christomodern hegemony. Sexuality is one such "factory installed" default program that drives modern coloniality through a guise of individual autonomy; race is another, though they function differently.

The concept of biopower also helps us identify ongoing colonial strategies even in contexts that might seem beyond the days of colony. In addition to whatever else it might yet

---

**32**   Cocks and Houlbrook, *Modern History of Sexuality*, 9.

be, Christianity in late modernity has become a regime of race, gender, and sexuality—a machine and a mechanism of raced and sexed biopower. Christian entities are constantly racing and sexing to messily secure control in a diffuse set of Christian hands, creating rough boundaries of civility and decency. These boundaries are profitable, and they serve to delegitimize the claims of others while protecting the claims of those who position themselves ideologically in proximity to the "god" of the regime.

While old-fashioned colonialism presents itself as governmental control of territory, today's Christian colonization runs on the hegemonic regulation of bodies, until finally to be Christian is not to follow any of the early creeds but rather to affirm certain types of bodies and scripted ways of acting in them. Merry Weisner-Hanks's study of Christianity and sexuality in early modernity captures a stage in this process. For example, Weisner-Hanks writes of early modern Christian colonization of Latin America, "Along with explaining the theological and spiritual concepts central to Christianity, missionaries also attempted to persuade—or force—possible converts to adopt Christian sexual morality; in many areas, after baptism, following Christian patterns in terms of a person's marriage rituals and sexual demeanor became a more important mark of conversion than understanding the Trinity or transubstantiation."[33]

The control we identify is overt as we look back on early modern colonialism; sexual teaching and its enforcement

---

33  Weisner-Hanks, *Christianity and Sexuality*, 181–82. So too Jordan points out that the Trinity is far less likely understood by contemporary Christians than various church rules about sex! See Jordan, *Ethics of Sex*, 5.

colonialism

was a direct mode of colonizer power over the colonized. But now, this kind of disciplinary control is often less overt as biopower. Rather the force now exerted as Christian teaching—or increasingly simply as "modern" life, or even as scientific fact—functions as a stealthy sovereignty, an ingested discipline. It functions as the regulation of bodies with unidentified benefactors, steadily producing binary, gendered bodies with complementary desire—that is, producing "men" and "women" and heterosexual binding; producing these as Christian in code for "white"; retro-projecting the divinity of this system, a white god, a paternal god, the spouse of the feminized church; and retro-projecting a very different set of meanings onto the way gender or bride imagery would have functioned in tradition before modern frames.

This gender system is an ongoing colonial complex. At once personal and political, this system not only informs our personal sense of identity but also can inflate national identity, as Ludger Viefhues-Bailey explores as he analyzes Christian defenses of the heterosexual binary and Christian sexuality "as a power-distributing and power-legitimizing system" in the US context.[34] Viefhues-Bailey finds that "the institution of romantic and respectable marriage is conceived of as the foundation of American society, and it helps discipline its citizenry."[35] This is an example of how biopower can circulate societally at vein level long after the more overt colonial postures of early modernity.

---

34  Ludger H. Viefhues-Bailey, *Between a Man and a Woman? Why Conservatives Oppose Same-Sex Marriage* (New York: Columbia University Press, 2010), 136.
35  Viefhues-Bailey, 122.

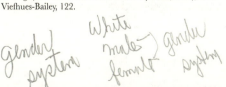

41

This pervasive control does show many of our familiar ways of knowing ourselves to be alloyed with forces less private than we might have thought. But this does not invalidate the actual pains we experience and the embodied struggles we know. Biopower does not mean that particular concerns related to sex and gender have suddenly evaporated or are shown to be an illusion. We know and feel these real, embodied struggles. For womxn's access to all we need to thrive in society. For womxn's safety at home. For capaciousness and access for LGBTQIA love and for social space so wide that even conflicting expressions of queer politics find a way forward. For flexibility and full societal access for everyone trans. For intersex recognition and flourishing. For an end to rape and sex trafficking. And more and more and more. An analysis of biopower does not mean that particular crises of sex and gender are not real embodied justice issues at this point—only that we cannot adequately address, counter, or transform them, especially as Christians, without first looking at the Christian role in quite literally engendering these crises.

Yet my interest here is not only to expose the biopower operations of the church in underwriting sexuality but also to query the bodily, political powers *otherwise* still possible for us as a church. I look for the church to queer its power, a process for which our Christology has already tuned us. We can practice other ways to flow as church amid a pervasive atmosphere of biopower. We might explore generative and nondominative power, our cocreative vocation, a process of which Christians are not in charge. We might be blessed to participate in a generative power from the people, a power that emerges not as power over but as revolutionary and improvisational from diffuse shared sites, sometimes a power with, sometimes a power for, sometimes a capacity as yet unknown.

## Theologizing Otherwise

Attending to questions of sexuality in the churches is not only about discerning our particular political positions, though it is most often treated as such: Christians who are politically progressive might attend to these questions to align their faith with their political agenda, or to seem to "include everyone" in the church and be welcoming. Meanwhile, Christians concerned about a "moral decay" in the progressive strands of Christian polity might attend to these questions in order to clearly label sins where they see them and present a corresponding set of moral teachings.

Yet attending to questions of sexuality in the churches is about more than these political positions that already exist for us and dictate our approaches to these questions in the first place. As we have already explored, it is also about attending to church misuse of power, especially as biopower. Further, to a large extent it is also about attending to the constraints of our own theological imaginations that the habit of biopower has shaped in us. This is what my home church member Doris foregrounded for me in her question years ago.

Unquestionably, the most significant crisis around sexuality and the churches is the harm done by the churches to countless individuals in distinct and separately unique ways. And then after this, related directly to it, is the ecclesial and theological crisis: not only that our church life has been limited as we exclude people from our churches and train ourselves in systems of harm but also that our views of God have been shaped accordingly, to the point that we testify largely to a false god of harm. We are losing touch with the vibrance of human communities and also the vibrance of the wideness of God.

Our attention to these questions is reshaped when we start from a recognition that in many of our Christian conversations about sex, we are being driven by issues Christianity itself framed. The fusions of coloniality and Christianity have shaped Christianity into embodied power patterns that we no longer easily recognize. We are meanwhile unknowing agents to further modern biopower productions, but we could alternatively divest of these strategies.

We can attempt to interrupt the bioshaping mechanisms, in terms of both race and sexuality, that Christianity fuels in today's world. We could replace these with the incarnation patterns more congruent with our gospel. This is something that should concern progressive and conservative Christians alike, because so long as we are invested in biopower, we are all distracted from what it is to be church. We are complicit in (bio)systems that are at the least not central to the work of the Christian gospel. We are thus draining an enormous amount of our collective energy into a counterproductive project; it is like a power leak wherein our generators are fueling something dangerous that we slowly built and then forgot how to live without. But I suspect the problem is much greater still, and we are not only losing power to a dangerous secondary project but rather fueling a project that ultimately

44

corrodes our primary one, a project that is antithetical to the work of the Christian gospel. Out of shared commitment to this gospel, liberal and conservative Christians alike need to divest ourselves of our entanglement in the sexing and racing work of modernity.

Heterosexuality is an artifice that upholds racial stratification. This stratification functions sharply, to a dehumanizing degree.

We embody these social structures. While it is analytically helpful to scrutinize them as systems, they don't exist as systems apart from the fiber of our bodies. We are the matter that vivifies them, materializes them, even when the systems are deadly for us.

While it may sound like these claims are novel to me, especially if these ideas are new to a reader in the churches, both the connection of heterosexism to racism and the emphasis on the body as a container for political realities have been discussed already. My contribution here is to press these conversations toward the churches, both to raise self-awareness of the complicity of Christian systems in these histories and to encourage Christian embodiments otherwise, that we might vivify more life-giving and fertile possibilities for this earth, and that we might incarnate the Christ of our name.

## Identity: But This Is Who I Am!

I am myself writing from within social identity categories and am cognizant of the significant social power of them: I'm a white cisgender woman and academic, writing in English in the United States. Complicatedly, I write about

cisgender = gender at Birth

45

queerness as a woman drawn to men (which is not yet to say, *straight*); I write about race as a white-bodied person, while holding myself, accountable to my ancestors from Europe, Africa, and North America.

The embodied life I've lived will limit and shape what I say here; at times, I've wondered if I am an inappropriate author here—as a white cis woman who has partnered men (and an ordained Christian at that!). Can or should write at all of the queer darkness of a sacred otherwise to Christo-modern contamination? This queer darkness so inspires me, and surprises me nearly every day with its insistent holiness, but should I attempt its praise, as me, when others can and will praise it better? I take the risk of deciding yes, because to yield to the social identities I receive as options (categories like "straight") without renegotiating them and improvising against their constraints is to remain faithful to the oppressive categories that delineate me and you and thus to fail my theological project at its root. A necessary breaking faith with oppressive categories is integral to the task undertaken here: man, woman, white, "homosexual," and heterosexual are all master's tools. I will try not to let those categorial tools control what I write here. I'm sure I will err at times.

I am also thinking with care of how this discussion of identities might land with you, as a reader. In making the argument that Christianity has shaped what we know to be "heterosexuality" and "homosexuality," I am also, as is by now clear, stating more basically that these categories of sexuality—and to some extent categories of bisexuality and asexuality, or at root, the whole category of "sexuality" itself—are social constructions of power before they are individualized parts of our personalized identities.

Yet for many who understandably and vitally need to claim a solid identity category in order to survive daily and relentless social oppressions (oppressions that simultaneously produce the available categories), my argument may feel threatening, even if I intend a more capacious social world for all of us. Our identity categories, especially when developed as resistance to oppression, are often, rightfully, a matter of pride.

Despite my identity-jostling words, I hope you will read on with me. There is still *bios*—life—after and amid biopower. Your body, your pleasure, still *is* in this moment, and my argument does not intend to jostle that. Meanwhile, oppressions need not set the terms of who we are; Christian hegemonic oppression certainly has no business doing so. We need a new vocabulary for subjectivity not published by the legitimized press of coloniality.

Make new words with me. Teach me what they are.

# 2

## Circulating Christomodern Power

That the "science of sex" seems to have come right at the end of Christendom or of a Christian age can trick the mind into absenting the church from that science. But it is also the case, of course, that many of the fields and forces of the late modern West are in some part shaped by Christianity. That "Christianity" is not present in ubiquitous cultural branding does not reveal Christianity's absence so much as its success in infiltrating a cultural ethos so sufficiently as to be nearly undetected. This Christianity is less a faith and more a hegemonic cultural gelatin.

To what extent is Christianity responsible for the production of sexuality in the modern West? A quantitative answer would be hard to prove, and there are clearly other forces like economic capital, medicine, and government deeply involved, though those forces again link back in the West to Christian colonizing power. Given the overwhelming social power of Christianities in the modern West and the manifold examples of Christian messaging on sexuality, a qualitative conclusion is hard to dispute: Christianity is to a large extent responsible for the production of sexuality in the modern West, and to a greater degree than most contemporary Christians admit or realize. Which is also to say, the production continues, even now.

Is it enough then for Christians to realize that Christian forces helped frame modern sexuality and thus to note the problematic irony in churches engaging the issues of sexuality as secular or biological rather than by-products of their polity? Such recognition alone does already help interrupt our discourse around sexuality in the churches.

However, the early modern production of sexuality is also directly connected to the contemporary ongoing Christian production of sexuality, which is not benign. People of the churches need to ask ourselves, Do we mean to participate in this modern machine, this power machination?

Deeper reflection on how Christianity fuels the regime of sexuality gives us direction on how we might resist and practice our faith otherwise. In this chapter, I pursue that deeper reflection. How has sexuality come to seem like an internal characteristic of who we are? In what ways has it simultaneously become an element of personal and social control? How does it interlock with categories of race and gender? In what ways is it an expression of the inner code of colonial power? What are the concrete impacts on bodies today, the ways in which this system of sexuality does daily violence?

## Sexuality as a Thing You Have

The modern sense of sexuality seems deeply personal, a part of our unique individuality. Individual "sexuality" has come to seem like it's tucked behind your belly button somewhere: part of you, personal, truly yours.

Yet if it wasn't always there (and to many of us, it will feel certain that of course, it was always there!), then how did it get in there? I am arguing that the church helped put it there. The church is complicit in the production of the Christomodern self and a Christomodern sexuality, and I call it by that name to underscore that complicity. Christomodern power effects an incarnation of imperialism through a colonization of the body itself.

Marcella Althaus-Reid offers a stirring example of how fixated Western Christianity has been on sexuality as something naturalized to the human body: "One of the challenges presented to theologians when reflecting on bisexual mountains and rivers, or on the whole sexed universe of the Andean people, is that in Christianity sexuality is strongly defined around the praxis of genitalia. If rivers do not copulate and give birth, or if they do not have orgasms, how can they be bisexuals (or male or female)?"[1] Driven by a Western Christian framework—thinking of sexuality as an innate component of human personhood expressed by specifically human bodies and genitalia, part of the recipe of a human self—how could we imagine the sexuality of a river? It becomes easy to conflate sexuality with a personality

---

1    Marcella Althaus-Reid, *The Queer God* (London: Routledge, 2003), 120.

structure, the person's "sexuality." This has become a "natural" way to think, and it can be hard to dislodge.

Lodged within, "sexuality" has become a deeply familiar and dominating contemporary Western framework. In their discussion of sexuality's modern history, Cocks and Houlbrook write, for example, of the Clinton-Lewinsky scandal: "For many observers, an individual's sexual behavior clearly said something about their character—it was an essential component of their very self."[2] Cocks and Houlbrook concisely summarize Foucault's diagnosis of this situation: "The notion that our desires, and particularly our sexual desires, represent the core of the self and the key to the personality, is, Foucault says, *the* defining feature of sexuality in the modern age. How, he asks, did it become possible to say that we have 'a sexuality', when previously there had simply been a mass of desires and practices, licit or illicit?"[3] This mass of desires and practices has now been bundled up, tidied up, and reconceptualized as an interior structure of selfhood.

I'll turn more directly to Foucault later in this chapter, along with the work of J. Kameron Carter, María Lugones, Mark D. Jordan, and others. They all help to turn our attention to biopower and the way Christian social forces are implicated in its production and maintenance, particularly under the terms of sexuality, gender, and race. I focus here most directly on sexuality, but the terms are not fully separable.

---

2  Cocks and Houlbrook, *Modern History of Sexuality*, 2.
3  Cocks and Houlbrook, 6.

Like race and gender, in the modern West, sexuality has gotten under our skin. And under the newly coined terms of *heterosexuality* and *homosexuality*, terms first used in the 1800s, it becomes not an aggregate of acts but "the symptom of a psychological state which govern[s] the rest of the personality" and even "the secret to the understanding of inner being and the mysteries of the unconscious."[4] Sexuality becomes very important and very powerful! As David Halperin writes, the modern situation is such that "sexuality is thought to provide a key to unlocking the mysteries of the self, even for *my* self: that is, I can explore and discover what my sexuality is."[5] At the same time, it becomes harder to observe, now shifted conceptually into our inner depths. The result, Halperin explains, is that "we now live, so the argument goes, with a model of personality centered on sex. Sexuality represents the most intimate feature of an individual, that dimension of the personality which it takes longest to fathom and which, when finally known, reveals the truth about much of the rest. A sexuality is a thing and I can have one."[6] A "sexuality" has become a thing, and one you should have—a key to who you are. This idea of sexuality as essential to selfhood reveals much about modern power, though the essentialism of the concept itself makes the social power harder to perceive.

Comparing the contemporary to antiquity, as Halperin does, throws into sharper relief just how novel the idea of sexuality as an inner structure of personal identity

---

4    Cocks and Houlbrook, 9.
5    Halperin, *Before Sexuality*, 5.
6    Halperin, 5–6.

is. Halperin writes that "one of the currently unquestioned assumptions about sexual experience which the study of antiquity calls into question is the assumption that sexual behavior reflects or expresses an individual 'sexuality.'" And while this may seem a benign assumption, in fact it harbors major meaning. We have now come to use the concept of "sexuality," as Halperin summarizes, in reference to "a positive, distinct, and constitutive feature of the human personality, to the characterological seat within the individual of sexual acts, desires, and pleasures—the determinate source from which all 'sexual expression' proceeds."[7] Far from a set of acts or desires, sexuality is now a "characterological seat" of self!

Halperin explains that "sexuality in this sense is not just the modern interpretation of sex, on a par with the (different) ancient interpretations of sex," but instead "a new category—central and centralized."[8] As such, sexuality is now doing a good deal of conceptual work for us: "It endows each of us with an individual sexual nature, with a personal essence defined (at least in part) in specifically sexual terms."[9]

Recall in contrast the erotic symbolics behind Romans 1, explored in chapter 1 through the lens of Stephen Moore's hermeneutics. Bodily virility, specifically symbolized by the erect man of social status (called *vir*, he puts the *vir* in

---

7  Halperin, 259.

8  Halperin, 6.

9  Halperin, 259. Halperin especially emphasizes here that modern "sexuality" is distinct from ancient Greek conceptions in "the autonomy of sexuality as a separate sphere of existence" and "the function of sexuality as a principle of individuation in human natures" (259).

today's *virility*), is the token of supreme social power. And in this system turned theological, God for these early Christians is also hard and penetrating. Note that this economy is *not* about someone's sense of self, their orientation, or their inner personal wants. It is not in you; it's on the lamppost. It is a public matter. (And women's embodiment doesn't appear on this scene.)

By now, we have come a long way from the phallus in city architecture. In contrast, individual sexual architecture is now so familiar that we in the churches have generated innumerable Bible studies, devotionals, disciplinary documents, ethical teachings, and theologies around them. Thus the churches continue to participate in implanting this chip of control within us, creating agonies of introspection, social conditions of exclusion, unlivable lives. Asked to respond, we offer Christian responses, which can only be superficial if we are not at the same time drawing attention to the chip and its implantation. Even in our most liberal or progressive teachings, if we are still assuming the structure of individual inner sexuality, we are not divesting ourselves of the Christian colonial postures that put it within us and feed on its placement.

Halperin notes that "sexuality is not a somatic fact, it is a cultural effect."[10] Thus, as a cultural effect, sexuality is not primarily a physical node tucked behind your belly button or

---

10   Halperin, 257. Halperin elaborates, "According to Foucault, sexuality is not a thing, a natural fact, a fixed and immovable element in the eternal grammar of human subjectivity, but that 'set of effects produced in bodies, behaviors, and social relations by a certain deployment' of 'a complex political technology'" (Halperin p. 416 in "Is There a History of Sexuailty?" in *The Lesbian and Gay Studies Reader*, 416-432; here Halperin is referencing volume 1 of Foucault's *History of Sexuality*.).

in your heart or perhaps in your genitals, though it may feel just that innate and personal. Confusingly, however, cultural effects do seep into the body. They become somatic, reshaping our embodied lives. Anne Fausto-Sterling discusses this phenomenon fully, most especially in her exploration of the way cultural concepts of binary sex in turn shape the medical management of intersex bodies.[11] The cultural can determine the somatic. Cultural effects have scalpels and direct impact on not only what we understand as biological but also how we in turn create the biological.

Our bodies, all the way to any imagined "core," are the primary template of the cultural. This means our bodies and their imagined core are vulnerable to social control, yes; it also means that they are our most proximate means of immense creativity. We can embody possibilities otherwise than the inherited scripts. That creative potential is the subject of the next chapter; here I continue to scrutinize the productions of Christomodern biopower.

*having power over Bodies*

## "Technologies of Individual Domination"

Christianity not only passed on its legacy of words on sex, a wordy inheritance that many readily recognize, but also helped concretize the idea of the inner self. In time, the programming chip of sexuality could have a nest; biopower's power plays are hidden from view in this interior cradle.

Foucault develops this idea as the interiorizing technology of the Christian pastorate. Jordan explains how

---

11    Fausto-Sterling, *Sexing the Body*.

"on one level, Foucault sees the Christian pastorate as the prelude to modern European governmentality."[12] Foucault is working with two kinds of confession, of "showing the truth about oneself"—that of faith and that of "who one is, of one's state."[13] Foucault is most interested in the second.[14] That confession of the self itself becomes the heart of a Christomodern subjectivity. As Jordan explains, "What distinguishes Christianity, Foucault says several times, is not the invention of the fall but of its repetition."[15] Again and again, we confess ourselves, performing subjectivity through confession.

On the most basic level, Foucault is pointing to confession as a Christian rite overseen by clergy, as with a confession of sins to a priest for absolution before receiving the elements of Eucharist. Notice, in this gatekeeping of the mass and the demand of personal disclosure, the assumptions of church control. Note the church's inspection of what will become introspection. It is as though in looking together at a thing—the self—it eventually takes a more solid form through the force of the inspection.

---

12  Mark D. Jordan, *Convulsing Bodies: Religion and Resistance in Foucault* (Stanford, CA: Stanford University Press, 2015), 131. Jordan offers an intricate analysis of Foucault's conceptualization of Christianity, and one that should be read before or alongside Foucault's posthumously released draft of *History of Sexuality*, vol. 4, *Confessions of the Flesh* (New York: Pantheon, 2021), along with a reading of Carter, who considers Foucault's potential recapitulation of Christian supremacist positioning of Judaism.

13  Jordan, 135. Also compare with Foucault in Michel Foucault, Luther H. Martin, Huck Gutman, and Patrick H. Hutton, *Technologies of the Self: A Seminar with Michel Foucault* (Amherst: University of Massachusetts Press, 1988), especially page 48.

14  Foucault et al., 48.

15  Jordan, *Convulsing*, 136.

Looking back on his discussions of "the technology of domination and power," Foucault himself confesses that now he is "more and more interested in the interaction between oneself and others and in the technologies of individual domination, the history of how an individual acts upon himself, in the technology of the self."[16] These technologies are intimate. They are much more intimate than you might expect a social scheme to feel. And that's just what makes them so pernicious and hard to track. These are "technologies of the self, which permit individuals to effect by their own means or with the help of others a certain number of operations on their own bodies and souls, thoughts, conduct, and way of being, so as to transform themselves."[17]

With a disturbing image of the ways we become prison guards of our own sense of self, in some places Foucault "speaks of self-observation as surveillance, the key word for the prison as Panopticon," in *Discipline and Punish*. As Jordan explains, this self-surveillance constructs "a vertical relationship of the self to itself."[18] We come to patrol the edges of our own territory, convincing ourselves through the patrol that it is our own. The self gets tucked inside these barbed fences of guarded selfhood. Safely behind your navel, it is then hard to believe anyone else has any say over what is so centrally "yours."

Thus Foucault observes a story of how Christianity—through confession, through the pastoral role in confession—came to establish a new role of the self to the self. Or, we

---

16    Foucault et al., *Technologies*, 19.
17    Foucault et al., 18.
18    Jordan, *Convulsing*, 137.

could say, came to establish an individual self: for that kind of cellular division into individuated false autonomy is indeed what happens through a turn away from more common identity into a vertical posture of surveillance on your own soul.

Next, however, the church's original programming is adopted for use in another newly forming modern category, the sciences: "From the eighteenth century to the present, the techniques of verbalization have been reinserted in a different context by the so-called human sciences in order to use them without renunciation of the self but to constitute, positively, a new self."[19] To stay with the technological metaphor, when the sciences download and run the church's self-surveillance program, they disable that part of the programming that had absorbed self-confession into an expansive mystagogy, those old Christian and Jewish themes of personhood as encountered and transformed by the divine and by an embodied peoplehood. And as Foucault writes of technologies of self now run and even guarded by modern sciences, "to use these techniques without renouncing oneself constitutes a decisive break" from the earlier function within the Christian pastorate.[20]

The internal sense of self, which is yours, which you patrol, is not "yours." This is likely not because of some productive relational coalition through which you "do" selfhood—which we could celebrate—but because of social

19   Foucault et al., *Technologies*, 48–49.
20   Foucault et al., 49.

control, the engineering of the self, social control for which we become cosigners in doing our own self-work.

Giving an indication that we are not forever resigned to control via biopower, Foucault gestures toward resistances or struggles that have been considered marginal and speaks about how "these processes, these unrests, these obscure, limited, and often modest struggles are different from the forms of struggle that have been so strongly valorized in the Western world under the mark of revolution."[21] Whereas that revolution would have aimed for a "total liberation, and an imperative struggle demanding in short that all other struggles be subordinated to it and depend on it," Foucault brings attention instead to different struggles, struggles that "target a form of power that has existed in the West since the Middle Ages, a form of power that is strictly neither a juridical nor political power, nor an economic power, nor an ethical domination, and that nonetheless has had large structuring effects within our societies."[22]

Important to my argument here, Foucault concludes, "This power has a religious origin." It is Christian power, and Foucault describes it specifically as "pastoral power." Its domain is the whole of a person's "individual" trajectory: "It is a power that aims to conduct and guide men during their entire life and in each circumstance of their life, a power that consists in taking charge of the life of men in their detail and their progress from their birth up to their death, in order to constrain them to behave in a certain way an ensure their

---

21  Michel Foucault, "The Analytic Philosophy of Politics," *Foucault Studies* 24 (June 2018): 196.
22  Foucault, 197.

Salvation. That's what we could call pastoral power."[23] It's a power of internal shepherding, a shepherding of the self. Again, Foucault diagnoses it as a Christian conception: "It is with Christianity, with the church institution, its hierarchical and territorial organization, but also the ensemble of dogmas . . . and with the definition of the role of the priest, that the conception of the Christians as constituting a flock has appeared."[24]

This Christian pastoral power functions not just to constrain individual action but also to shape the sense of self itself, to expose subjectivity and "structure the relationship" the person has with their "own conscience." Both of these, constraint of action and conscience control, are enacted in the name of salvation. This is the substance of Christomodern subjectivity. Foucault describes it as an "individualizing power," involving "an obliged relationship of oneself to oneself in terms of truth and compelled discourse."[25] The "pastorate" is a word for shepherds, and Christomodern biopower shepherds subjectivity itself.

The church develops this individualized conception before late modern structures and professional fields will invoke it as an obvious given and will seek to inform and shape it apart from church affiliation. Thus eventually, Christomodern subjectivity becomes culturally embedded in a subtle enough form that a person could receive a psychoscientific diagnosis related to sexuality, experience the somatic impacts of this diagnosis, and pay for it through an insurance system, all

23   Foucault, 197.
24   Foucault, 197.
25   Foucault, 198.

as a personal and nonreligious matter, while meanwhile there is a subtle Christian political system underneath—in the categories invoked for subjectivity and sexuality and in the posture of reflection and analysis on the self.

Thus Foucault speaks of "a whole redeployment, a whole transplantation of what had been the traditional objectives of the pastorate" that occurred as "capitalist and industrial societies as well as the modern forms of the state accompanying and supporting them found themselves in need of the procedures, the mechanisms, essentially the procedures of individuation that the religious pastorate had put in place."[26] Modern society runs on the "procedures of individuation" produced in the church. Again, this is why I dub them *Christomodern*—so that we cannot overlook the Christian underpinning of a modernity that would pose as free of its religious roots. As Foucault observes, even after much of the overt religious connection would be modified, "there was an implantation, even multiplication of the pastoral techniques."[27]

Foucault is certainly not the only one to point to the function of interiority in the modern Christian conception of self. Charles Taylor emphasizes the sense of interiority in the modern self, and traces its development, but without Foucault's methodology (and in some disagreement with it).[28]

---

26  Foucault, 199.

27  Foucault, 199.

28  Charles Taylor, *Modern Social Imaginaries* (Durham, NC: Duke University Press, 2004), 193–94. He returns to this theme in *A Secular Age* (Cambridge, MA: Harvard University Press, 2007). In his *Sources of the Self*, he issues critique of Foucault and "neo-Nietzschean thinkers." Taylor, *Sources of the Self: The Making of Modern Identity* (Cambridge, MA:

Taylor traces the theme of interiority as one of the hall-marks of modernity given by Christianity in the West. Taylor presents "a history of modern identity," by which he means "to designate the ensemble of (largely unarticulated) understandings of what it is to be a human agent: the senses of inwardness, freedom, individuality, and being embedded in nature which are at home in the modern West." Within this, he focuses on three major dynamics, the first of which is particularly relevant here: "Modern inwardness, the sense of ourselves as beings with inner depths, and the connected notion that we are 'selves.'"[29]

In analyzing secularity, Taylor determines that there is still a sense of God or Spirit, only not where people might have traced them before "a secular age." Taylor writes of a "shift from the enchanted to the identity form of presence." Here "God or religion is not precisely absent from public space, but is central to the personal identities of individuals or groups, and hence always a possible defining constituent of political identities."[30]

Though Foucault and Taylor both diagnosis a focus on interiority, ultimately, they disagree about its meaning. What in Foucault is a site of inner disciplinary power is for Taylor a potentially helpful locus of the divine. It is as though the mostly bad for Foucault is the potentially good for Taylor. And while Foucault will theorize ways that bodies can resist this subjugation, Taylor views Foucault as someone hopeless

---

Harvard University Press, 1989), 71, 99–101, 490. Taylor reads a kind of unconscious universalism in Foucault, an "impossible neutrality" (519).

29  Taylor, *Sources of the Self*, ix.
30  Taylor, *Modern Social Imaginaries*, 193–94.

in outlook. For our study here, it is significant simply that both Taylor and Foucault note not only a modern sense of individualized interiority but, crucially, a Christian role in forming it.

Giorgio Agamben also emphasizes the imprint of Christianity on the construction of modernity. Yet as Claire Blencowe writes, "The thrust of at least some of Foucault's arguments is all but inverted in [Agamben's] *Homo Sacer*."[31] Similar to the way Foucault's more constructive vision for what might happen with bodies that resist is missing from Taylor's analysis, so also Foucault's understanding of bodies in resistance has a positive side and an empowering side that Agamben misses.[32]

Alexander G. Weheliye analyzes a critical and telling shortfall in both Foucault and Agamben's use of biopower: they exercise a kind of colonial amnesia.[33] They eclipse the role of colonial power in shaping modern biopower and thus too easily ignore that modern biopower is fundamentally *racializing*. Weheliye makes clear that biopower cannot be clearly seen while neglecting to see race.

In appropriating the biopower concept for my argument about Christomodern control, I aim to emphasize the full colonial fusion of race, gender, and sexuality. These seemingly separate concepts are all one colonial technique for producing bodies. I turn now to the fused racializing and

---

31 Claire Blencowe, "Foucault's and Arendt's 'Insider View' of Biopolitics: A Critique of Agamben," *History of Human Sciences* 23, no. 5 (2010): 114.

32 Blencowe, 118, 127.

33 Alexander G. Weheliye, *Habeas Viscus: Racializing Assemblages, Biopolitics, and Black Feminist Theories of the Human* (Durham, NC: Duke University Press, 2014). See particularly 61–65 and 47–48.

gendering functions of Christomodern biopower and its prized artifact of "sexuality."

## The Personal Is Political Control

Where does this internalization of social power take us? Into the body. Thus, while Foucault's overall concepts of disciplinary power also apply to the way Christomodern control has functioned, biopower in particular most precisely names the embodied nesting of this control. This is a power inlaid in our biology. It is not a biological given, but it becomes a biological experience.

Disciplinary power is wider than biopower, and so too is colonialism. Colonialism does not flatly equal biopower: even in modernity, there are many other ways of taking and making a colony. Yet when scrutinizing the way Christianity has implanted internal controls through categories like sexuality and race, we can say that these make of the body a colony. These make of the soul someone else's territory. Thus this is biopower. (And like plastics that linger in the body's tissues long after the substance is declared toxic and the manufacturing halted, biopower lingers in a way that other disciplinary powers might not, such that decolonial efforts to rid one's people of biopower, or the postcolonial out workings of biopower, are never pure, indeed are often productively impure.)[34]

---

34 For one exploration of the generative productivity of anticolonial resistance, see Ashley Dawson, *Mongrel Nation: Diasporic Culture and the Making of Postcolonial Britain* (Ann Arbor: University of Michigan Press, 2007).

As "biopower," colonizing powers have shifted onto the terrain of the inner body, internalized in selfhood through Christian colonial codes of race, sex, and gender, never in isolation from each other.

At first approach, the concept of biopower can sound like a flat synonym for socialization. As such, it can sound not modern at all but rather age old. Yet the term intends something more pernicious than more general cultural socialization. Thus Cocks and Houlbrook explain that while some have described modernity as a tale of liberalization and freedoms, "Foucault inverts this story of progress." Modernity instead utilizes a stealthier form of control. Foucault traces this story of increased and insidious control, not modernity's louder trope of freedom. Cocks and Houlbrook emphasize that in the shift to biopower, "the result was that while modern people became freer from the terror of the state and its capricious authority, they nevertheless came to be endlessly calibrated, their capacities endlessly judged, their productivity endlessly rated, their normality and pathology eternally measured."[35] This calibration rose in terms of sexuality, yes, and also race and gender.

With biopower, social control shifts to the terrain of the inner self, which we want to hide from security cameras and where we least suspect outside social interference. Even from the church. The "inner" is thus the ideal container for social control: we own it as "ours," we turn off our awareness of outside surveillance because we carry out the surveillance ourselves. We become the keepers of our own colonized state.

---

35 Cocks and Houlbrook, *Modern History of Sexuality*, 8.

Unlike other ways of talking about dominating social power, biopower (perhaps best captured by underscoring the *bio* in Foucault's term) is, as J. Kameron Carter explains, "power as refracted through certain 'scientific' conceptions of human biological processes," such that late in modernity we behold "power's transition" from power enforced through early modern nations to power's "instantiation through *bios* or bare life itself."[36] As such, "biopower" conveys that "in the modern modes of power, 'bodies and what they do' are the field over which power operates."[37] As Cocks and Houlbrook emphasize about this transition of power, "the result was that while modern people became freer from the terror of the state and its capricious authority, they nevertheless came to be endlessly calibrated, their capacities endlessly judged, their productivity endlessly rated, their normality and pathology eternally measured."[38] Race, gender, and sexuality are interrelated units of this calibration.

Thus, while there are many examples of socialization, and many types of dominating social power, biopower uniquely emphasizes control on the geography of "bare life itself," on the human body and the selfhood simultaneously located there. Whereas an analysis of socialization is likely to consider the role of culture or a specific society in that socialization, biopower appears to *transcend* any cultural specificity by means of the body—a transcultural, global terrain. No matter what society socializes you, the physical body appears as

---

36  Carter, *Race*, 60.
37  Carter, 63.
38  Cocks and Houlbrook, *Modern History of Sexuality*, 8.

a (falsely) universal or cross-cultural terrain.[39] Race, sexuality, and gender appear, wrongly, to transcend cultural differences. That people seem to "have" a race and a sexuality, no matter where they live, is a trick of biopower.

As the territory of power becomes the body itself, race becomes a primary category, a new foundation, indeed a founding category of modernity, as J. Kameron Carter makes clear.[40] Carter, whose work elaborates on the fundamentally theological nature of this process, describes how "race comes to work in a decentralized and deterritorialized way" and "begins to articulate itself within the global flows, communications, and currencies of power—flows and currencies that exceed any one nation's borders."[41] Race becomes a very furtive, very wide disciplinary power. As noted earlier, Weheliye explores the shortcomings of analyzing biopower without central attention to race. Weheliye calls out the segregation of the field—the way in which the theoretical discourse of biopower from the likes of Foucault and Agamben is often separated from the discourse of critical race studies.[42] So too Carter writes that Agamben "takes us to the scene of a glorious production, the production of Europeanization and the glorious theo-logics of that

---

39 Carter writes that as this territorial shift is effected through biopower, "fulfilling the Enlightenment's quest for cosmopolitan universality, the territory of power becomes *bios* or life itself and in its totality" (*Race*, 60).
40 Carter, 60.
41 Carter, 60–61.
42 Weheliye, *Habeas Viscus*.

production, while yet repressing the complementary process of non-Europeanization."[43]

Carter's appropriation of Foucault directly appraises the relationship of race and disciplinary biopower. And as I said at the outset, it was Carter's *Race: A Theological Account* that made me own Christianity's complicity in the modern frameworks in which we live: colonized frameworks that are at once racializing, sexualizing, and gendering. So much of my activism or my liberative teaching efforts strained within these categories of race, sex, and gender, searching for just ways to approach them as a Christian, as though justice could be realized within them. Once I saw the categories as not only problematic but foundationally produced by Christian coloniality, my approach to justice had to shift.

Carter makes obvious how "modernity's racial problematic" has significant "theological depths" and how the "problematic of whiteness" can be understood as a *"theological* phenomenon."[44] Carter's work explains the way in which "modern racial discourse and practice have their genesis inside Christian theological discourse and missiological practice, which themselves were tied to the practice of empire in the advance of Western civilization."[45]

A less precise (though still vastly important) claim is more familiar: that race was constructed by Christian colonizers in

---

43  J. Kameron Carter, "The Inglorious: With and Beyond Giorgio Agamben," *Political Theology* 14, no. 1 (2013): 81. Carter continues sharply, *"Homo sacer*ization, then, not means something quite materially and somatically specific that is lost to view in Agamben's text, but that nevertheless haunts the text" (81–82).

44  Carter, *Race*, 6.

45  Carter, 3.

early modernity as European colonizers forced their Christian frameworks onto those they enslaved and colonized. Yet Carter makes a more specific and incisive point, taking his readers to the roots of racism in Christian supersession of Judaism: "For at the genealogical taproot of modern racial reasoning is the process by which Christ was abstracted from Jesus, and thus from his Jewish body, thereby severing Christianity from its Jewish roots."[46]

As Carter explains it, the Christian supersessionist categorizing of Jewishness (summed up as the theological discourse of the "Judenfrage" or "Jewish question") "functions as the constantly ramifying inner mechanism that propels modernity and moves its discourse of race."[47]

Thus the point that Christian colonialism constructs the modern category of race cannot be adequately made without examining theologically sustained Christian violence against Jews. Theologically—not only politically or biologically—and with genocidal consequences, Christian bodies have been constructed in supercession to Jewish bodies, bodies split into racial categories. Race emerges through theological supersession as a category of suppression and oppression, stratification, and white supremacy.

Carter thus argues for race at the base of the other categories modernity has constructed. Carter writes, "The deep structure of the problem of sexuality as a vector onto life itself in the production of modern subjects, of modern man, is race, and it is race that links the different forms of peoplehood

---

46  Carter, 6.
47  Carter, 44.

in early and late modernity, respectively."[48] Carter demonstrates that the Western Christian construction of categories of racial supersession—the categories that will structure modernity—is achieved through a theological procedure of abstracting Jesus from his body. A disembodiment of Christ is the theological recipe for racist Christomodernity.

Carter presses his readers to face the problem of "what is religious about modernity and the way it parodies theology at the same time that it cloaks this fact." He writes that "the discourse of race is critical to the cloaking process and thus functions as a vital cog within modernity's own religious and quasi-theological machinery." When this cloaking is ignored and the pseudotheological character of modernity passes in hidden costume, modern mechanics of bodily control succeed most smoothly. Thus failing to recognize the "cloaking," as Carter writes, "not only leaves the problem of modern racial reasoning inadequately understood but also can yield responses that risk—unwittingly, no doubt—reinhabiting, at the politically unconscious, theopolitical level, the very problem that needs overcoming."[49]

In the field of theology, Carter notes the dearth of engagement with the modern and uniquely theological problem of race. This is not to say that there are not theological accounts, many of them rich, of the effects of racism or the churches' participation in or resistance to racism. Yet while race is recognized as a modern concept, it is less frequently recognized as a concept that is in large part

---

48  Carter, 60.
49  Carter, 40.

*Problem with Race*

theologically produced.[50] It is not simply that the churches have been racist or have produced resistance to racism but rather that Christian theology is at the root of the oppressing function of race in the first place. It is an account of that kind of Christian complicity, and its effects on the health of theology, that Carter offers and which he sees that theology, including much Black liberation theology, has neglected.[51]

Similarly, there are many compelling theological responses of sexism, and some of heterosexism. And there are vivid examples of theological resistance to sexism, and again sometimes heterosexism. But sexism and heterosexism present a crisis for contemporary theology not simply because they are manifestation of systemic sin or evil in the world to which faithful Christians must respond but because sexuality is a product of distinctly Christian power. It's integral to Christian coloniality.

Yet with hazards similar to that of invoking race in the field of theology without recognizing its theological roots, sexuality is too often overlooked in theological work as a Christomodern production. While heterosexism, and the sexual system behind it, is sometimes at least recognized in theology as a uniquely modern Western concept, it is less frequently recognized as a concept that is in large part

---

50 Thus, Carter concludes, "It is precisely in grasping what is theological about the modern condition generally and about the modern problem of whiteness in particular that one finds so little assistance in the work of so many that have taken on the modern problem of race" (377).

51 Carter finds that Black theology does not adequately analyze "the problem of race, its arising and maintenance, as theological and religious in character" nor show "the convergence of the religious-theological and cultural-political dimensions of the problem" (387n4; see also 43).

Christian in its making. Yet resistance to coloniality's victimization means recognizing sexuality as such.

Thus the "cloaking" problem that Carter diagnoses with the pseudotheological nature of the concept of "race" also happens with sexuality. It is very easy to miss the pseudo-Christian character of sexuality. It can seem an obvious thing—a falsely obvious thing—that we live in a time of free sex, not Christian religious influence and control.

Mark Jordan helps us remove the cloak. Contributing to a colloquy on "feminism, sexuality, and the return of religion," Jordan writes, "What makes us think that Christianity ever left? Since the Enlightenment, since Revolutions, the disestablishment of certain churches or regnant theologies has been confused with the banishment of religion because 'religion' only meant a certain enforcement of Christendom." Jordan points to the way Christianity continues under our skin: "Christianity continues to occupy languages and bodies, to instruct aspirations and habits, long after its churches are disestablished and its theologies ridiculed."[52]

The ongoing occupation of languages and bodies has much to do with "sexuality," for, as Jordan writes, "if anything was supposed to prove our freedom from dead churches and their ridiculous theologies, it was our *orgasmic* enlightenment, our *sexual* revolution," and yet clearly "that sexual 'liberation' did not silence the discourses of a once-dominant Christianity or quell its political outbreaks."[53]

---

52 Jordan, "Return," 40.
53 Jordan, 40; emphasis in the original.

Calling back to mind Halperin's description of modern sexuality as a "characterological seat," Jordan too describes a seat. Jordan recalls the "premature announcement of God's death by Nietzsche's madman" and notices that "the cultural place of the Christian God, the throne of the old lawgiver, is still not empty." In a magnificent cloaking not unlike that described by Carter, on the throne of that thundering old God now sits none other than "King Sex."[54]

Jordan writes, "Instead of confirming Enlightenment and Revolution, the death of God not only made a void into which sex could enter, it fixed the conditions for sex to take power as sexuality." Using *Him* deliberately to refer to the God of this discourse, Jordan writes that "the absent God has been replaced by a Sex trained during His long reign and emboldened by His temporary absence. This Reign of Sex is only possible after the Christianity of Christendom."[55]

It is a reign fueled by biopower, in which it seems to me that King Sex has a simulacrum of his throne embedded under the navels of all his subjects. King Sex is, as Jordan writes, the "viceroy" of the old king, of Christianity.[56] Thus, Jordan concludes, "Christian discourses about sex are now and at once the vanquished predecessor, the constant alternative, and the chastened collaborator of discourses about sexuality. There is no way to draw the genealogy of these relations except as incest. Christian discourses about sex are parent, sibling and child to the

---

54  Jordan, 40. The appellation "King Sex" was Foucault's (see Jordan, 40n1).
55  Jordan, 40.
56  Jordan elaborates that "the old king spoke sex too—indeed, practiced his power originally through cunning, curious ways of talking about sex" (41).

discourses of sexuality."[57] To return from the scene of this messy throne room to the premise with which I began this book: Christianity is complicit in making the "sexuality" to which it is forever responding and that it is regulating in overt and "cloaked" ways.

Far from benign, the implications of Christomodern power constrict human bodies and constrict whatever beauty Christians could have. The viceroy King Sex is not good for bodily flourishing: "Pronouncing the death of the Christian God meant introducing a better-sexed divinity—but also divinizing better-managed *human* sex."[58] As for the churches, Jordan summarizes the suffocating situation succinctly: "[Christianity] under the regime of sexuality is barely Christian, most especially when it shouts out its fidelity to the categories of sexuality."[59]

Overall, race and sexuality both bear a Christian theological character, too easily overlooked. Carter's diagnosis that "theology came to function differently in becoming a racial discourse" resonates with Jordan, who writes, "In one sense, modern sexual identities remain intrinsically theological both in their genesis and their logic. They arise out of Christian pastoral or canonical discourses, and they carry over the rhetorical tropes that make it possible to build a

---

57  Jordan, 47.
58  Jordan, 41. Jordan diagnoses a significant stricture around sex: "For Foucault . . . sexuality closes a syntax around sex much more tightly than Christianity ever could" (47). Evidence of such tight regulation of sex is now affirmed by the volume David M. Halperin and Trevor Hoppe, eds., *The War on Sex* (Durham, NC: Duke University Press, 2017), discussed later in the chapter.
59  Jordan, "Return," 53–54.

morally decisive role around sexual desire."[60] These factors, as we will explore next with María Lugones, can also be identified in gender itself.

## "Gender Does Not Travel"

Even after we do the tricky conceptual work of shifting ideas of race and sexuality and understanding them as distinctly Christomodern categories, gender can seem like a category left safe from this analysis. One thinks that surely gender is older, and indeed, there have been ways of categorizing human bodies into types that we could call "gendered" apart from Western modernity. Yet there is a specific kind of gendering that goes together with Christomodern race and class in the "colonial/modern gender system" theorized by Lugones.[61]

Lugones offers "a framework to begin thinking about heterosexism as a key part of how gender fuses with race in the operations of colonial power."[62] With Lugones, it becomes clear that race, sexuality, and gender are fused: she emphasizes that they more than intersect—they interlock.[63]

---

60  Carter, *Race*, 6; Jordan, "Return."
61  María Lugones, "Heterosexualism and the Colonial/Modern Gender System," *Hypatia* 22, no. 1 (Winter 2007): 189.
62  Lugones, 186. Lugones's stress on the intrinsic entanglement of multiple oppressions resonates with Laurel Schneider, "What Race Is Your Sex?," in *Disrupting White Supremacy from Within*, ed. Jennifer Harvey, Karen A. Case, and Robin Hawley Gorsline (Cleveland: Pilgrim, 2004).
63  Lugones is critical of theories of intersectionality; she finds them insufficient.

Lugones argues that colonialism did not impart earlier European ideals unmolded. Rather, "it introduced many genders and gender itself as a colonial concept and mode of organization of relations of production, property relations, of cosmologies and ways."[64] Sexuality, race, and class are key components for understanding gender in modernity; colonial gender is fused with them both and thus does not exist in its contemporary form before those other, distinctly modern concepts. When overlooking all this, Lugones laments that "the heterosexualist patriarchy has been an ahistorical framework of analysis."[65]

Lugones grounds her work in the feminisms of women of color and of the Global South,[66] and she historicizes gender firmly in its colonial context. And as we have been exploring here, it is impossible to accurately narrate modern Western colonialism without underscoring that we are telling a *Christian* story.

Lugones presses feminist theorists especially to see that gender is a colonial product, daily reproduced by coloniality, with gender itself a system of reproduction.[67] As the editors

---

64 Lugones, "Heterosexualism," 186.

65 Lugones, 187. She laments, "I have seen over and over, often in disbelief, how politically minded white theorists have simplified gender in terms of the patriarchy" (188). Without taking into account colonial power when thinking about gender, we keep scrutinizing "a binary, hierarchical, oppressive gender formation that rests on male supremacy without any clear understanding of the mechanisms by which heterosexuality, capitalism, and racial classification are impossible to understand apart from each other" (187).

66 Lugones, 187.

67 Lugones, "Decolonial," 747. She names her terms: "My intent is to focus on the subjective-intersubjective to reveal that disaggregating oppressions disaggregates the subjective-intersubjective springs of colonized women's agency. I call the analysis of

of a volume in her honor explain of Lugones's system, "the priority given to heterosexuality in the colonial/modern gender system" both turns people into animals and makes white women into reproducers of whiteness and wealth, white capital.[68] This is "coloniality"—reducing people to classifications in this way.[69]

Christian colonizers, encountering civilizations, did not enter conversation; rather, "the process of colonization invented the colonized and attempted a full reduction of them."[70] The colonized become "de-souled specters of the human."[71] The denial of humanity equates to coloniality; coloniality is the denial of humanity, and it "emerges as constitutive of modernity."[72]

Coloniality is not black and white; rather, Lugones diagnoses a colonial situation of the "light" side and the

---

racialized, capitalist, gender oppression 'the coloniality of gender.' I call the possibility of overcoming the coloniality of gender 'decolonial feminism'" (747).

68  Pedro DiPietro, Jennifer McWeeny, and Shireen Roshanravan, eds., *Speaking Face to Face: The Visionary Philosophy of María Lugones* (Albany: State University of New York Press, 2019), 15–16.

69  Lugones, "Decolonial," 745. She draws her understanding of coloniality as it relates to dehumanization from Nelson Maldonado Torres, *Against War: Views from the Underside of Modernity* (Durham, NC: Duke University Press, 2008). She draws "coloniality" from Anibal Quijano ("Colonialidad del Poder y Clasificacion Social," *Festschrift for Immanuel Wallerstein*, part 1, *Journal of World Systems Research* 5, no. 2 [Summer/Fall 2000]: 342–86). For Quijano, "coloniality" is not the same as colonialism, as colonialism does not necessarily involve racist power. But neither is coloniality a phenomenon limited to race: "Coloniality does not just refer to racial classification. It is an encompassing phenomenon, since it is one of the axes of the system of power and as such it permeates all control of sexual access, collective authority, labor, subjectivity/intersubjectivity and the production of knowledge from within these intersubjective relations" (Lugones, "Heterosexualism," 191).

70  Lugones, "Decolonial," 747. This is a reduction "to less than human primitives, satanically possessed, infantile, aggressively sexual, and in need of transformation" (747).

71  Lugones, 753.

72  Lugones, 749; cf. 745.

dehumanized.[73] And that which is "de-souled" or nonhuman cannot be gendered, cannot be heterosexualized.

Under coloniality, there are no humans on the dark side, and thus there is no gender on the dark side. And the only sexuality present is the paring of the light pair, "man" and "woman." Queer and dark are nonhuman under coloniality. Humanity exists on the light side, where gendered men and women are found: "Sexual dimorphism became the grounding for the dichotomous understanding of gender, the human characteristic."[74]

Hence Lugones will stress that gender and heterosexuality and race cannot be disentangled. They are not simply intersectional. Their intersections, together with that of class, do not fit within the categories of modernity.[75]

They are interlocked and mutually saturating: "biological dimorphism, heterosexualism, and patriarchy are all characteristic," Lugones explains, of "the light side of the colonial/modern organization of gender."[76] The light side is civilized, and "only the civilized are men or women."[77] They are also Christian.

Again stressing that the intersections of the categories reveal an enmeshment larger than modern categories can hold, Lugones explains that "if woman and black are terms for homogeneous, atomic, separable categories, then their

---

73  Similarly, in Carter's work, "white," "race," and "black" indicate more than color: "They signify a political economy, an *ordo* or a social arrangement, what Irenaeus calls an *oikonomia*" (Carter, *Race*, 8).
74  Lugones, "Decolonial," 744.
75  Lugones, 742.
76  Lugones, "Heterosexualism," 190.
77  Lugones, "Decolonial," 743.

intersection shows us the absence of black women rather than their presence."[78] Thus Lugones makes the startling claim that "the semantic consequence of the coloniality of gender is that 'colonized woman' is an empty category: no women are colonized; no colonized females are women." Therefore, Lugones declares that "the colonial answer to Sojourner Truth is clearly, 'no.'"[79]

Resonating with Gumbs's phrase, "racialized, ableist heterocapital," Lugones concludes that "global, Eurocentered capitalism is heterosexualist." Heterosexuality only exists at all as a product of coloniality and as a production regime for it. Lugones writes poignantly that we must see the violence of the construction: "I think it is important to see, as we understand the depth and force of violence in the production of both the light and the dark sides of the colonial/modern gender system, that this heterosexuality has been consistently perverse, violent, and demeaning, turning people into animals and turning white women into reproducers of 'the (white) race' and 'the (middle or upper) class.'"[80] Lugones emphasizes that "heterosexuality is not just biologized in a fictional way; it is compulsory and permeates the whole of the coloniality of gender in the renewed, large sense."[81]

From the angle of Lugones's work on coloniality, Christian colonialism clearly appears as the producer of modern sexuality. Plainly stated, Christomodern bioproduction makes straight white men and the women who reproduce

---

78  Lugones, 742.
79  Lugones, 745.
80  Lugones, "Heterosexualism," 201.
81  Lugones, 201.

them. Thus Lugones's analysis of the colonial/modern gender system draws us further than Foucault's biopower alone. It thus resonates with Weheliye, and it also resonates with the way in which Carter sees race as the animating principle behind Foucault's system.

Coloniality reveals the consequent workings of biopower: colonial power writes itself into bodies to the extent that it undoes particular embodiments. It delegitimizes and dehumanizes. Coloniality is a biological agent that undoes life.

The frame of coloniality helps reveal the devastating consequences of biopower. It is genocidal for most bodies. It redesignates human embodiment as the domain of a narrow few. It marks only particular life as worthy of grief, as "grievable" as Judith Butler might say it.[82] Coloniality relegates much life below the light side of that human regard. Christomodernity erases souls.

Yet Lugones does not suggest that we should therefore go about redistributing the light side into the dark. This is conceptually impossible because the light side is built on top of the dark; it stands on it and cannot redistribute into it, by design. All that inclusion or equity rhetoric could do here would be to reify the ultimate purity of the light side, by seeking to include more within its oppressive bounds.

So for Lugones, "the suggestion is not to search for a non-colonized construction of gender in indigenous organizations of the social." And this is because "there is no such thing; 'gender' does not travel away from colonial modernity."[83]

---

82   Butler, *Undoing Gender*, 17–39.
83   Lugones, "Decolonial," 746.

In this system, it becomes clear that gender categories are employed to create heterosexuality, as reproduction and as patriarchal control. In this sense, gender categories are intended to be patriarchal control. The category of man is reproduced on the category of woman, and the two are needed in order to build the normalizing structure of heterosexuality. Lugones's colonial/modern gender system throws into sharp relief disciplinary power embodied as gender, as heterosexualized gender. Gender becomes more obviously implicated than sexuality as a primary locus that exemplifies biopower.[84]

The structure of heterosexuality is held up as a structure by gender, and gender holds up a structure of race. Sexuality (as heterosexuality) holds up race (as white supremacy). Or conversely, white supremacy depends on heterosexuality to uphold it. Gender and sex give flesh to whiteness, show us what whiteness looks like and how it continues. Sexuality and gender ensure the disembodiment of Blackness and brownness and render Black and brown life inhuman.

At this point in chapter 2, therefore, the production manuals for gender, sexuality, and race are evident behind the Christomodern throne, even occupied as it is by a cloaked stand-in. Indeed, for Lugones, the role of Christianity in coloniality can hardly be overemphasized:

> Christian confession, sin, and the Manichean division between good and evil served to imprint female

---

84  As Chitty analyzes, sexuality has passed the "biopolitical threshold." See Chitty, *Sexual Hegemony*.

sexuality as evil, as colonized females were understood in relation to Satan, sometimes as mounted by Satan. The civilizing transformation justified the colonization of memory, and thus of people's senses of self, of intersubjective relation, of their relation to the spirit world, to land, to the very fabric of their conception of reality, identity, and social, ecological, and cosmological organization. Thus, as Christianity became the most powerful instrument in the mission of transformation, the normativity that connected gender and civilization became intent on erasing community, ecological practices, knowledge of planting, of weaving, of the cosmos, and not only on changing and controlling reproductive and sexual practices.[85]

Christianity is a primary agent in the dehumanizing transformations of coloniality.

Coloniality is lived out in our bodies, concretely. It is exhausting. Factory floors, bedrooms, and confessionals blur: "The coloniality of gender is sensed as concrete, intricately related exercises of power, some body to body, some legal, some inside a room as indigenous female-beasts-not-civilized-women are forced to weave day and night, others at the confessional."[86] Confessions to the priest, confessions to the colonizer, confessions to King Sex, confessions of the self that are not our own.

---

85  Lugones, "Decolonial," 745.
86  Lugones, 753.

## King Sex's War

It can still be hard to detect the Christianity complicit in sexuality, race, and gender. It is, after all, King Sex seated on the throne: Christianity seems positively medieval and provincial! But as explored earlier, the seemingly universal, deterritorialized, unbound nature of these categories is a crucial aspect of how they function. Once we see them as bound concepts, we can query who binds and who benefits. But recognizing that bound frame is difficult, counter-cultural work. It can feel like nonsense. Hegemony relies on it feeling like nonsense and actively polices it as such.

Along these same lines, identifying a Christian catalyst in the construction of race and sexuality can first appear like nonsense. One thinks, "Race and sexuality are really old. The issue is not how they came to be but how Christians respond to them now!" Or, "Race and sexuality are cultural products, but not of the churches. The churches lost power in modernity. Didn't you get the memo?"

I did get the memo telling me that church power is gone in modernity: the memo was a trick! Jordan got it too: "Triumph over Christendom has been a tenet in sexual politics."[87] King Sex has tricky propaganda. The churches continue to shape and constrict bodies through biopower in the colonial/modern gender system.

Christomodern power is cellular at this point, and hard to detect. This also means that when King Sex wages war, old King Church slides all too easily off the hook.

---

87   Jordan, "Return," 40.

And wars are on. David Halperin and Trevor Hoppe's edited volume, *The War on Sex*, shows the profound and pernicious continuing effects and workings of biopower. Despite marriage equality and many gains, contemporary America is too easily, and wrongly, read as a place of sexual freedoms. Halperin and Hoppe's volume shows how the levels of control and punishment are deep and multivalent, involving, for example, the criminalizing of various forms of sexual practice and expression. It seems that sex itself is the enemy.[88] And as Halperin writes in the introduction to the volume, this contemporary war "has had a particularly violent impact on those who are socially marginalized, socially stigmatized, or racially marked, or who cherish nonstandard sexual practices."[89] Halperin and Hoppe's volume also describes many ways in which progressive political movements and conservative political movements join forces in fighting sex. The huge numbers of "sex offenders" now registered in the United States show that disciplinary strategies relying on conceptions of individual sexual natures are common and distressingly widespread. As analyzed in that volume, as of 2015, there were more sex offenders registered in the United States than there are residents in the entire state of North Dakota. That sounds like absurdly many, but one might still assume that we simply have that many people with some inner problem—until, that is, one hears that 16 percent of convicted sex offenders are themselves under age twelve. This is not simply a list or a historical count: this

---

88  Halperin and Hoppe, *War on Sex*, 3 and 47.
89  David M. Halperin, introduction to *War on Sex*, 3.

is a disciplinary registry that marks people publicly as deviant. And the disciplinary measures taken on sex offenders are distressingly violent, as the authors of *The War on Sex* explore in detail. The authors also explore how transgender women of color are disproportionately met with punitive measures.[90]

Amid this perilous war on sex, in the spring 2021, and long after his death, Foucault was in the news at least twice. First, his family's decision to publish in English the fourth volume of his *History of Sexuality* (subtitled *Confessions of the Flesh*) brought it to the public even though Foucault had not wanted posthumous publications.[91] Second, and far more disturbing and significant, Foucault's own sexual exploitation of children was brought to the press by an observer.[92]

There is no defense of Foucault, nor should there be. From the account made public, it seems clear that Foucault

---

90  To further explore how this "war on sex" relies on punishment and in particular incarceration, see Eric A. Stanley and Nat Smith, eds., *Captive Genders: Trans Embodiment and the Prison Industrial Complex*, expanded 2nd ed. (Oakland: AK Press, 2015).

91  Foucault's *Confessions of the Flesh* works with the topics explored from Foucault in this present volume, concerning the role of Christianity in the production of modern sexuality and in particular the function of the Christian pastorate. It is derived from drafts left unfinished when Foucault died; the same topic in Foucault's work can be alternatively explored through the lectures and publications of his lifetime. Mark Jordan's *Convulsing Bodies* explores in careful detail the role of religion in Foucault across many of his texts and thus makes an excellent companion for anyone seeking to place volume four in the context of Foucault's arguments overall.

92  The observer, Guy Sorman, reports Foucault to have regularly paid young Tunisian children for sex. Sorman elaborates, "Foucault would not have dared to do it in France. . . . There is a colonial dimension to this. A white imperialism." Matthew Campbell, "French Philosopher Michel Foucault Abused Boys in Tunisia," *Sunday Times*, March 28, 2021, https://www.thetimes.co.uk/article/french-philosopher-michel-foucault-abused-boys-in-tunisia-6t5sj7jvw.

abused children. I do, however, want to defend our thinking from that which will shut it down when the topics of sex are raised. Sex panics can shut down our thought, especially because they engage the workings of biopower lodged within all of us. But we need to maintain our thinking capacity in order to interrupt the war on sex.[93]

For when the topic of sex as a "characterological seat" seems too personally pivotal, we lose much ability to think it through in terms of social power. We become less able to make distinctions between situations we hear of in the press involving, for example, children and sex. We need to maintain the analytical ability to make distinctions between situations such as, on the one hand, a powerful elite intellectual using money and colonial status to demand sexual access to children and, on the other, a situation in which two teens in love take pictures of each other naked. Because the latter scenario has recently received more public, legal punishment than Foucault ever received, our need for this distinction is critical.[94] When we think of sex acts as flowing from something "characterological," something fundamental

---

93    As Halperin articulates incisively in the introduction to *The War on Sex*, "There is no denying that sex can be a vehicle for harm, sometimes very serious harm. It is not only legitimate but indeed imperative to stop people from using sex to harm one another. Sexual freedom is not a license to abuse others for one's own pleasure. But preventing sexual abuse should not furnish a pretext for an all-out war on sex that permanently identifies sex itself with danger and with potential or actual harm. Nor should it provide a justification for dispensing with all measure and proportion in deterrence and punishment" (4).

94    Halperin and Hoppe's *The War on Sex* explores at length the recent legal punishments of minors convicted of sexual offense, sometimes absurdly charged with offenses against their own selves.

to character, we can too easily stop reading them and our response to them as signifiers of social power.

We need to resist the faux security of Christomodernity's purifying structures, including those that deem colonized Indigenous bodies to be heathen and those that repeat the colonizing and demonizing gesture with those corralled onto the sex offender lists.

We need to stay savvy to how violent the war on sex is in a supposedly liberated society. As Halperin writes of the current and perhaps unexpected war on sex, "In short, the familiar stories we have been telling ourselves about the sexual revolution, the rise of sexual permissiveness, the collapse of old-fashioned sexual morality, the change in sexual attitudes, the progress of women's rights and gay rights, the decriminalization of sodomy, and the legalization of gay marriage have all diverted attention from a less familiar but equally important story about the new war on sex, a war that in recent years has intensified in scope and cruelty." The impression that we are somehow getting free of oppression through sexual liberation or progressive politics is a dangerous illusion.

In the context of this volume, I want to emphasize this war as King Sex's war and reiterate that King Sex sits on a Christian throne. Christianity is waging daily war on bodies, at a cellular, cloaked level. And this while Christianity is also a story of divine power at a cellular level! The Christomodern war on sex is a horrid travesty of Christian incarnational potential.

Gayle Rubin has stressed the ways that discourses on sexuality such as those of the antiporn movements, in which feminists and antifeminist conservatives disturbingly collab-orate, are "less a sexology than a demonology."[95]

This war on sex is part of the deployment of what Mbembe terms "necropower." Mbembe charts the progression of bio-power all the way into a "necropolitics." Mbembe's analysis makes clear that modern biopower has become widespread necropower, leaving the globe under death-dealing sys-tems.[96] And as we have explored here, it is a death system underwritten by Christianity.

As I noted at the outset of chapter 1, the fixation of the churches on "sexuality" is an important indicator of the success of Christomodern power strategies. As I have by now explained, the Christomodern way of organizing and controlling bodies is an imperial strategy programmed as biopower, colonizing body and soul, and it infrastructures/architects the colonial/modern gender system. When we fix-ate on the categories of this system, particularly as a church, we not only play by the system's rules; we also fortify and further them. We do exactly what the system asks of us (though this is far from what a Christian gospel could ask of us).

Even more telling than our fixation on categories of the colonial/modern gender system is our violent enforcement of

---

95  Gayle Rubin, "Thinking Sex: Notes for a Radical Theory of the Politics of Sexual-ity," in *The Lesbian and Gay Studies Reader*, ed. Henry Abelove, Michèle Aina Barale, and David M. Halperin (London: Routledge, 1993), 28. This pivotal article was first pub-lished in 1984. There, Rubin also makes the critical observation that sex itself is a cate-gory of oppression: "Sex is a vector of oppression. The system of sexual oppression cuts across other modes of social inequity, sorting out individuals and groups according to its own intrinsic dynamics" (22).

96  Achille Mbembe, *Necropolitics* (Durham, NC: Duke University Press, 2019). Also see the discussion of Mbembe in Weheliye, *Habeas Viscus*, 63.

its terms, whether for gender, sexuality, or race. Necropower aimed at dark bodies is a powerful tell of the efficacy of the Christomodern power. Necropower aimed at trans bodies is a powerful tell. The evidence of annihilating violence fueled by the Christomodern "light" side against Black and brown bodies and queer and trans bodies is staggering. Any given week of work on this manuscript alone brings new examples of that violence. But what this book seeks to emphasize to Christians seeking to interrupt that violence is that this sexed and raced violence is deeply funded and structured by Christianity itself. It is Christomodern violence. Christians are complicit, not Good Samaritan first responders to the scene of this pain. Respond we must, but since the structures of Christian hegemony in the modern West are death dealing, our responses will need to deviate from those structures in order to be resonant with the life-affirming potencies of the Christ of our name.

It may seem ironic for me to label the war on sex that Halperin and Hoppe announce as King Sex's own war. Surely King Sex is bacchanalian, not militarized against nonconforming sex? But conforming is precisely King Sex's regime, and conforming can even seem a small price to pay, for in King Sex's court, you get to have your own sexuality and the pride of your own identity—it seems we need only conform to ourselves, so how bad can King Sex really be? Though it is hard to track, the Christomodern category of sexuality—that interior, privatized category with which I began this dispatch—is precisely a tool of biological warfare. This sounds drastic. Yet as we have already explored, it dehumanizes and demonizes and it criminalizes bodies and pleasures. The daily impacts are indeed drastic. Thus is the impact of a gendered, violent church.

The pernicious embedding of Christian control is like a silent programming operating in the modern Western individual, Christian or not. It is waging war. As is the way of war, it dehumanizes its victims and trains its soldiers to be embodiments of trauma. The victims: the inhabitants of the queer dark side. The soldiers: the men and women of the light side.

Christianity in the modern world has become a sexing and racing machine of vicious operation, tearing up lives and bodies. This kind of vicious control degrades and depletes what Christians could be tending for our world, those embodiments of healing and freedom promised in our Scriptures, beneficial power loose in the world through holiness incarnate.

## Conclusion: Instructions to a Complicit Church

I want my complicit church to stop circulating Christomodern power and assemble differently. Many days, the need seems so obvious to me that it seems a simple enough thing to ask. But I also imagine that were I to announce this want directly in most of the church contexts in which I find myself, it would sound like a very large and even confusing ask. Even for those eager to engage my argument, I recognize that thinking about biopower and coloniality can seem like a complex philosophical load, so much so that it's easy to muddle in that complexity and forget to apply this concept to the daily work of doing Christianity differently.

Thus we can back up again to where we started and review the argument in basic form: there is social power laden in the body. Taking that one step further, add the governance that is crucial to Foucault's understanding: there is governing power laden in the body. Your inner self becomes, paradoxically, the territory of social control. Taking another step, add surveillance: Your inner self is the territory of social control, now policed in service to governing norms most primarily by *you*. Biopower is social power in your private self for which you have taken up the maintenance, by default, likely unnoticed.

What are the terms of this power? They are *body* terms. They have to do with how you understand your body or how you are taught to do so. They have to do, in both a deeply piercing and boringly quotidian way, with race, sexuality, and gender. What is your race? (Which box will you check on the next form? What will your race mean, on the job or in health care? In what terms do you value the category of "your" race?) What is your sexuality? (Have you come out? Are you "straight" or gay? What will this say about you?) What is your gender? (And what is your unborn baby's "gender"? Have you painted her walls yet?)

Gender, sexuality, and race are social categories, surely. But they are also *embodied*. They are words about our *bodies*.[97] If you are discussing gender, sexuality, or race, you are discussing embodiment. And if you are discussing power in terms of gender, sexuality, and race, you are discussing

---

97 They are also in another sense words about our flesh, with all the theological resonance of that term. See Mayra Rivera, *Poetics of the Flesh* (Durham, NC: Duke University Press, 2015).

a power whose commerce is the body. Race, gender, and sexuality are not born of the body as biological givens, but they are born out on and through the body. They matter in ways we can touch and feel; they shape the contours of our births and deaths. They play out in actual material textures of experience, in suffering and in joy.

Gender, sexuality, race—to what degree are any of these things "yours"? They will surely feel *yours*. They will feel inside you. They will feel like "who you are." They feel like identity. But are the terms, the values, the categories, *yours*? Do they derive from you? Of these tangles, Judith Butler writes that we are always doing our gender for someone else. I do "my" gender as a currency of communication and flow in a system that is precisely not mine. Always as none other than a subject in a social world, my autonomy is undone; my own subjectivity is not my own. In some sense, the social possesses my self-possession.

While these ways that the social is embedded in one's "my" functions in pernicious and problematic ways, they also give us paths of exploring and utilizing our deeply social natures: As Butler writes, "We're undone by each other. And if we're not, we're missing something."[98] Our social nature is also inviting and generative, and we can utilize it. We can remake the social through innovation and improvisation that reshape shared horizons and make our common world more capacious.

Improvisation is possible. Acting otherwise is possible. Practices of freedom are embodied daily. We drag against

---

**98** Butler, *Undoing Gender*, 19.

the constraints of coloniality, we improvise in the tense openings upon which we insist, and as Butler says, in embodying fantasy and the unreal, "we bring the elsewhere home."[99]

We take up those possibilities amid a scene in which Christianity has been complicit in the racing and sexing of modern life. When we deliberate individual lives, acts, and sexualities, we are deliberating the direct object of Christian production, not the power holder itself. We need to analyze Christian power over and over—because it is operative over and over—and decide how to navigate as a church amid that kind of power play. We will need to stop church and theology for the sake of life abundant on this planet, or we will need to wrestle its capacities out of the juggernauts of the modern oppressions it has supported and foster the possibilities emerging from the persistent capacity of divine presence.

It is worth remembering that Christianity is possible without (and was possible before) its embedding in a modern sense of interiority. Concepts of interiority help conceal the biopower techniques of modernity, as we have seen with race and with sexuality, making them harder to detect and analyze. We may need to relearn how to do Christianity without reliance on essentialized interiority.

We can certainly learn, at least, how to do "sexuality" without interiority, or more properly—since the word *sexuality* itself goes alongside interiority—we can become agile with notions of bodies and pleasure that do not rely on interiority. The churches could begin to interrupt their claim on

---

99   Butler, 29.

biopower anchored in sexuality through a habit of continuously referring to bodies and pleasures without an essentialized interior dimension.

Such reference may feel initially like a loss, like the removal of a vital and familiar organ. But there are many ways we can explore both the discourse and the tactility of bodies and pleasures. The erotic can be more expansive than sexuality would have us believe. Rather than being a defining essence tucked away somewhere under your belly button, the sexual instead offers matrices through which you dance, tunnels and viscosities through which you can enter and withdraw, malleable cultural atmospheres you can reshape with the alchemy of your affiliations.

And though we in the churches may find this discussion of sexuality something better filed away under "interesting gender theory," this topic is church business too. We cannot separate Christianity from the modern Western transformation of personhood, this new conceptualization of the inner identity with a sexuality. This is a conceptualization of *control*. Far from a benign new category, it is suppressive and life reducing. Those of us captivated by a liberating and generative spirit in Christianity need therefore attend with particular care to the functions of sexuality among us: not primarily to the manifold news stories and moral deliberations about it but foremost to the way it provides an anchoring tether to ongoing Christian colonialism, within our bodies themselves, even within our sense of soul.

The Christomodern subject, the self with an interior domain, is not simply some product of years and years of philosophical evolution, as though it were some inevitability in Christianity, opening out from the Scriptures and the early documents of the tradition. Concrete actions on concrete bodies shaped our intangible sense of self. Actual concrete structures explain such a concrete result as embodied selfhood, and for that we have a plainly evident actuality: Christian imperialism and the forms it came to take in early modernity as a global imperial system of colonial control. Thus the Christomodern sense of self-interiority is not a philosophical development so much as a colonial product. We don't become convinced in theory of a new way of understanding our embodiment. We become convinced in the body. We become convinced by actions carried out on the body, by actions perpetrated by bodies: by the whip, the suffocating hold, the lynching tree, the rape, the excommunication, the erecting of missions and forts, the shattering of kinship structures, the desecration of graves and holy sites, the warfare, the murder. The Christian confessional alone might seem almost quaint and delicate in its effecting of a new subjectivity, but it is a confessional enforced by colonial weaponry. There are locks on its doors and high, concrete costs for its refusal.

Of course, the philosophies and theologies of the Christian empire will support a modern sense of self and show the transition into it, but this sense of self comes to be primarily not through that discursive evidence of philosophical teaching but through a concrete commerce and a brutalization of bodies.

It is not a Christian response to sexuality that we need be worried about. It's the other way around. Rather, modern Western sexuality is instead a response to Christianity—a violent product of it. We Christians need to decide, not what we will say about sexuality, but what we will do about our gendered, violent church, this racing/sexing/gendering machine that functions at a frenetic pace, forming bodies and marking many as disposable. Theologically, we can ask what else is possible: What role might the scattered body of Christ have in bringing forth shared embodiment otherwise?

# 3

# Assemble Otherwise

One semester in class with my students, I challenged us to draw a timeline across the board: "a sketch of Christianity in relation to colonization." We discovered that by the end of it, in order to figure out what to sketch, you have to consider Christian wielding of the tools of race and sexuality, whereas in earlier times you might have looked at wielding of the sword, land, and governmental edict, even if justified in terms of faith and confession.[1] Christian colonialism has a longstanding tradition of creedal enforcement.

We started with the time of Jesus's life, before Christianity was a thing, before the big category of Christianity as a "religion." We wrote down, "Jews as a colonized people under the Roman empire" and "Jesus, a colonized Jew." We sketched Jewish movements against empire. We noted how Jews were alongside other groups of colonized people, and how some people from these various groups came into the

---

1   Peter Brown, *Power and Persuasion in Late Antiquity: Towards a Christian Empire* (Madison: University of Wisconsin Press, 1992).

Jesus movement as one among other anti-imperial communal groups. We circled for emphasis "colonized people" and "anti-imperial."

Next, we sketched the complicated multivalent story of Christianity as colonial strategy: a "Christianity" that already in its earliest colonial iteration had seen multiple divergences, multiple strands of this tradition that would go on to exist apart from Roman imperial Christianity (such that Christianity has always been plural, "Christianities," despite empire's attempted erasure of this plentitude and difference). We added to our timeline the colonization of western Europe, where the sacred oaks turned crucifix, as Rita Nakashima Brock and Rebecca Ann Parker recount.[2] The long and multiple crusades. And then early modern enslavement ships and the Christian colonies. Christian missionaries, Christian enslavers. Also, enslaved Christians, singing in Christ an old anti-imperial song.

And then, we pause with our sketching markers in hand. How do you draw the modern relationships of Christianity to colonialism? Christian power continues to colonize, even where old signs of "Christendom" seem to have faded. One way to track this—to sketch it for our study—is to consider biopower and, increasingly, necropower, considering the ways that our bodies are shaped, constrained, legislated, and even deemed disposable by the norms of this religious enterprise. The colony is now our skin and our bedroom. By the end of the sketch, you are drawing yourself.

---

2   Rita Nakashima Brock and Rebecca Ann Parker, *Saving Paradise: How Christianity Traded Love of This World for Crucifixion and Empire* (Boston: Beacon, 2008).

Christian colonization has resulted in a tragic co-optation of "the body of Christ given for you." And yet, somehow still, it is in these same bodies that we can do Christianity otherwise. We will do Christianity otherwise with our skin, sweat, and joy; with our skin, sweat, and joy we enflesh the kin-dom of God today, provisionally, emergently, with those others who find the current dominative machinations of Christianity incongruent with the Christ of our faith. We reclaim the agency of our bodies—a repetitive practice, not a reclaiming accomplished once and for all. We will need, again and again, to take back our flesh from the Christo-modern regime of colonial power in order to reclaim the vital medium of our bodies, to reclaim the medium of embodiment on which the incarnation comes into play ever again in our world.[3] We can practice sacramental assembly in the fissures of empire. And thanks be: bodies have never stopped doing so, even when so many bodies conformed to or were subsumed by colonial shaping.

To sum up where we have been so far before this final chapter: That which looks in the West like the fall of religion and the rise of scientific society can also be understood conversely as a widespread colonial implantation of Christian values and of theologically underwritten political power. The current discourses around sexuality and the churches are iterations of a later moment in that discursive project;

---

3   It is a plural, plentiful incarnation, or as Laurel C. Schneider names it, promiscuous. See her chapter "Promiscuous Incarnation" in Kamitsuka, *Embrace of Eros*, 231–46. For another constructive theological resourcing of promiscuity, see Elijah Nealy, "Who Do You Say That I Am? Transforming Promiscuity and Privilege," in Talvacchia, Larrimore, and Pettinger, *Queer Christianities*.

they are not at root examples of the churches responding to nonchurch issues. The operations of Christian maintenance of sexuality—bodily programs running through our sense of self—are one of today's most powerful Christian colonialisms, rooted in the body as colony. Current discourses around race and gender are inbred with sexuality and are all presently operative Christian colonialisms.

Meanwhile, the circulation of holy power in the world continues about its play. Seeking to tap into, celebrate, and amplify that holy power, Christians can and do improvise many forms of coalitional sacred practice, resisting necropower and multiplying beneficial power in varied unpredictable forms.

In this final chapter, I gesture toward possibilities for resistance in theologizing otherwise. I write here in the form of musing, not of conclusion and certainly not of prescription. This chapter is purposely lyrical and nonconclusive. Those seeking firm argument and conclusion will be unsatisfied, but those parameters mimic coloniality too closely to engage them here. Closure is not the gesture here; opening is.

While a chapter is simply a chapter, I would like the form to fit the subject: Christic subjectivity, whether ecclesial or more personalized, remains inconclusive, inspiring transformation, not solidity. The christic has always been otherwise.

Yet in ways already explored here, Christianity—in its multiple embodiments as institutions, as persons, as social artifacts and structures—has been deeply caustic to the Christ of its name. As Jordan reminds us, "If an analysis of power is going to do more than repeat power's own propaganda, it must be able to unmask it so as to make it less tolerable."[4] However, rather than making biopower intolerable, Christians can too easily further it with their talk and teachings on sexuality as individuals and institutions. After all, biopower is deeply embedded in our social and personalized embodiments. It has become default.

So far, I have been seeking to unmask for church people the propaganda map of "sexuality" for which our church has been a behind-the-scenes cartographer. You might say in affirming response, "Very well! I will no longer let church powers control what I think about my sexuality!" Yet it is precisely this idea that free of exterior power, inside yourself, you have a sexuality of your own that is itself the old furtive way that church power exerts an ongoing control. To disrupt Christomodern biopower, we have to dislodge the idea of sexuality as an essentialized interiority, as a discrete characterological seat of self, not simply help ourselves exercise self-control over it (which is what many churches say they want anyway).

Christians need to release their fixations on "sexuality" while still promoting health to bodies and their pleasures and reducing harm, especially for those most vulnerable. Christians will do this not by teaching sexual ethics differently but through a different way of being a Christian assembly, by no longer being church as arbiters of disciplinary biopower but as coalition sites for other forms of emergent power.

And meanwhile, there are other ways we can conceive our bodies and pleasures apart from a characterological seat of

---

4  Jordan, *Convulsing*, 110. Also see 114–15.

our personhood. For example, we might think of the sexual as a kind of communitive aesthetic saturating the world, across many contours of place and form. Such a "sexual" is both bigger than a human personality structure and at the same time smaller, *not* a fundamental element of person-hood: a driver of the world's artistry but not of the self.

Theorizing resistance to empire among the multitude, Michael Hardt and Antonio Negri write that "the ethical horizon has to be reoriented from identity to becoming." Their horizon of "becoming-other" is deeply resonate with Butler, whose work on precarity they engage. Hardt and Negri write, "History isn't then ever just a story of domina-tions but also of resistances to biopower."[5]

Likewise in Christian history, throughout and despite Christian hegemony, Christian people somewhere have always found ways to improvise against that hegemony. The work of improvisation is old, though the improv itself is always freshly emergent. There is no once-and-for-all form of resis-tance to perfect and crystallize as rubric.

Accordingly, in *I Want to Be Ready: Improvised Dance as a Practice of Freedom*, Danielle Goldman stresses that Foucault prefers "practices of freedom" over "liberation."[6] The term *liberation* gives the false impression that a finished goal or

---

5   Michael Hardt and Antonio Negri, *Commonwealth* (Cambridge, MA: Belknap Press of Harvard University Press, 2009), x and 31. They further explain that Foucault's primary attention is on "the power over life—or really, the power to administer and produce life," and yet "there is always a minor current that insists on life as resistance, an other power of life that strives toward an alternative existence" (57).

6   Danielle Goldman, *I Want to Be Ready: Improvised Dance as a Practice of Freedom* (Ann Arbor: University of Michigan Press, 2010).

state will be achieved, when in fact, freedom requires steady improvisation. It requires freeform action.

In keeping with this idea, Christian practice otherwise than the fueling of Christomodern power is not any once-and-for-all conversion so much as a steady readiness for creativity against the friction of what the church does as coloniality. Practices otherwise than coloniality are a thing people do; they are not a thing a bishop or a committee decides in advance on their behalf, though a bishop (or even possibly a committee!) can also be a body in practice, and an inspiring one. For collective ecclesial subjectivities, as for more personalized ones, practices of freedom will be ongoing ways of devising and revising subjectivity and presence against the constraints society will place on the self, on what can be "yourself." Our selves, as well as our polity and ecclesiology, will need to be improv.

Following the cues of Lugones's framework for the colonial/modern gender system, we can anticipate that these practices will be embodied on coloniality's pluriform dark sides: these practices emerge as dark and queer improvisations of proactive sacrality. These provisional practices embody ecclesiologies otherwise.

In using the word *otherwise* to describe ecclesiologies here, I am echoing it appreciatively from the way it has arisen in Black studies and Native and Indigenous studies, particularly as explored in *Otherwise Worlds*, edited by Tiffany Lethabo King, Jenell Navarro, and Andrea Smith.[7]

---

7    Tiffany Lethabo King, Jenell Navarro, and Andrea Smith, *Otherwise Worlds: Against Settler Colonialism and Anti-Blackness* (Durham, NC: Duke University Press, 2020). See especially the chapters in this volume by Ashon Crawley and J. Kameron Carter.

## Ecclesiologies Otherwise

Christian assembly otherwise does not equate to the large project of Western decolonization. Assembly otherwise is plural, certainly, but decolonization is radically more plural and a vastly larger scene. It is importantly, needfully, not always Christian. Christian assembly amid the multitude is more specific; it is one way that bodies collide and sanctify in the fragile autonomous zones carved out in the interstices of empire.

Christian assembly otherwise is not sheer decolonization; rather, it participates in decolonization and is also Christian *ekklesia* (meaning assembly, in Greek, and the root for ecclesiology). Assembly otherwise is an improvisational ecclesiology. It is sacrament practiced in decolonizing zones. It is an embodiment. It is the making and marking of sacred body in spaces where sacrality has been long and lastingly desecrated. It is not a return to a pure past. It is a fresh incarnation with the contaminated matter of now. It will be different tomorrow.

Hard to recognize and chart, near impossible to rubricate, these incarnations nonetheless sing with the cadence of Mary's song: the mighty fall from thrones, the hungry are filled, and sacredness gestates. Sacredness stirs within and emerges anew in broken and vulnerable sites, like a dark stable in colony's crevice, where birth stimulates an early assembly of mother and magi and shepherd.

Assembly otherwise, *ekklesia* otherwise, is an eruptive, emergent, interruptive ecclesiology, a body of Christ known fragmentarily. This is admittedly problematic for anyone trying to maintain an institutional church. It makes it tricky to ordain and difficult to codify into sacramental guidelines. It might, on the other hand, not be so difficult on catechesis because it is deeply participatory. It relies on many acting bodies who take up assembly, not on the leadership of one cleric. In the language of mutual aid and abolition, "we keep us safe." Perhaps because collaborative agency is key, Christian formation, whether of adults or of children, might come more easily in this improvised and emergent ecclesiology.

This precarious ecclesiology introduces, in its ephemerality, heightened vulnerability. Old systems of deterring or disciplining abuse or shaping preparedness for ministry and leadership will have been disrupted. Thus this precarious ecclesiology will call for a higher level of widespread or commonly owned responsibility, a kind of lay accountability. In this improvisational ecclesiology, one cannot rely on the presence of someone trained or schooled in best practices for preventing harm. Instead, harm prevention and reduction will have to be more widely shared areas of knowledge and skill.

In the spread of sacrament beyond the control of previously institutionalized ecclesiology (noting of course that Christian sacrament has always also existed beyond these controls), improvisational ability replaces rubrics for how and when to proceed. Improvisational ability is harder; it's more demanding in that it requires presence and attentiveness to the constraints and needs of the present moment. It is also for that reason often more delicious and vibrant.

When embodying sacrament in coalitional assembly, the same factors guide any who are taking it up in the same way that clergy should have always been guided in the church: things like assurance of consent and resonance with the relational web present in a given assembly, including its ancestral lines and its visions of the future, its Scriptures and art forms, and invocations of holiness that themselves can disrupt even the assembly's own intended disruption, invocations that are an openness to transcendence even if that transcendence comes from below or beside.

It is in the same bodies that serve the mechanics of biopower that we also have the musculature to do otherwise. This is evident in the way Foucault discusses biopower: while Foucault emphasizes the controlling governmentality of the Christian pastorate, he also elaborates "forms of resistance internal to the pastorate."[8] He will enumerate five of them and elsewhere reconsider them; they include, for example, ascetical practices and countercommunities.[9] Thus while Foucault stresses governmentality, Foucault also wants to explore alternatives arising within it.

Jordan's meticulous and affectionate study of religion and resistance in Foucault helps describe the resistance theme that emerges across Foucault's disparate writings, lifting up "the recurring image of the appearance of a new form of power in the interstices of the old." Jordan highlights in Foucault not only the "heterotopies"—or the spatial interruption of a "getting outside" of modern technologies that can be read in Foucault—but also temporal ones: openings within time, heterochronies.[10] Thus when Foucault concludes the

---

8  Jordan, *Convulsing*, 130.
9  Jordan, 31; also see his related footnote number 23 on that page.
10  Jordan, 166.

first volume of *The History of Sexuality* with an invocation of "one day" to come when "in another economy of bodies and pleasures one will no longer understand very well how the ruses of sexuality . . . succeeded in submitting us to the austere monarchy of sex," Jordan reads a temporal interruption of subjectivity, or an atemporal emergence of it: "One day: this is a time marker for alternative subjectivation."[11]

Sacred assembly otherwise can also be read as "heterochrony." These openings of difference are possible and emergent even within Christomodern domains. They are tense and temporary portals. They crack time open to what Lugones calls the "non-modern." Lugones uses "nonmodern" to highlight the way in which modern logic would have us label such other time as "premodern" and thus less enduring, less relevant for interrupting the now, less threatening to the current epistemic regimes.[12]

The portals of otherwise may be perceived as breaks in time, as with a heterochrony, or also in space—a heterotopy. Different theorists testify to these multiple possibilities in multiple ways. Elizabeth Freeman writes of time and queerness.[13] Fred Moten writes of Blackness and space.[14] Willie James Jennings writes of the spatial disruptions of colonialism and the formation of race that flows from this

---

11  Jordan, 165.
12  Lugones, "Decolonial," 743.
13  Elizabeth Freeman, *Time Binds: Queer Temporalities, Queer Histories* (Durham, NC: Duke University Press, 2010).
14  Fred Moten, *In the Break: The Aesthetics of the Black Radical Tradition* (Minneapolis: University of Minnesota Press, 2003).

displacement.[15] Or as Harry Maier theologically explores as he weaves Foucault's heterotopia with Michel de Certeau's "notion" of tactics, "tactics" can involve "the appropriation of time and space for unconventional and idiosyncratic ends."[16]

In addition to space and time, the "otherwise" might also be described as a rupture in sound. Reading all the resistant or "convulsing" bodies in history that Foucault revisits in his writings, Jordan admits that "a reader might conclude that Foucault is pious about those convulsing bodies"—and indeed, decides Jordan, "he is. His piety urges him to find a form for registering their sounds."[17] Foucault is drawn to resistant embodiments of subjectivation, their possibilities and their pleasures. Jordan describes that "for Foucault, the most arduous writing recalls scenes of bodily resistance at the edges of language. The scenes are often religious in superficial ways. They are more deeply religious in structure, so far as they evoke the ritual or liturgical time of transformation. Religious writing isn't defined by its subject matter so much as by its liturgical alteration of bodies in time."[18] Bodies resist. What are the sounds of the heterochronies of liturgical alteration of bodies in time? What are the syncopations of the otherwise? What sensory interruptions

---

15 Willie J. Jennings, *The Christian Imagination: Theology and the Origins of Race* (New Haven: Yale University Press, 2010).

16 Harry O. Maier, "Soja's Thirdspace, Foucault's Heterotopia and de Certeau's Practice: Time-Space and Social Geography in Emergent Christianity," *Historical Social Research* 38, no. 3 (2013): 83. Maier develops a theological vision of the emergence of the kingdom of God across these various time/space interruptions.

17 Jordan, *Convulsing*, 199.

18 Jordan, 199.

fissure coloniality's grip, and what sensory resonance brings incarnation home?

A most vivid intimation of otherwise sound comes in the writing of Ashon Crawley as he celebrates the non-normative space of blackqueer joy. Particularly in the tonal, vibratory quality of Blackpentecostal worship, Crawley hears these sounds of resisting bodies and traces the liturgical transformation of bodies. What, Crawley asks, "can the vibration-as-sound and song emanating from the Blackpentecostal worship space tell us about life and love as queer horizon and thrust?"[19]

Perhaps it tells us how any kind of assembly otherwise is possible. Crawley testifies, "The presence of blackqueerness makes possible the very practice of praise and worship."[20] This is because "blackqueerness, like nothing music, is the zone from which emerges the normative but also, importantly, the infinite range of possibility otherwise than the normative. The infinite range of otherwise possibility, the infinite range of plurality, is the space of the social, the space of the common and commons, the space of the popular and the criminal. . . . The point is the practice against the normative in the service of life's flourishing."[21] Crawley hears the "nothing music" of bodies in praise amid a kind of heterochrony. Let Crawley's description assure the reader of the tangible reality of the otherwise. A fantasy world, yes, but one already practiced and made physical in embodied praise and its sweat and tears, its claps and its voice.

---

19  Ashon T. Crawley, "Susceptibility," *GLQ* 27, no. 1 (2021): 13.
20  Crawley, 15.
21  Crawley, 27.

Crawley's description of blackqueer praise gives a vivid example of assembly otherwise that insists on being other than coloniality's dehumanized, unpeopled ground. Assemblies otherwise exceed the categories of their designated possibility. They are emergent human/divine incarnation. Assemblies otherwise are the musculature of daily salvation, of ebullient, insistent generative life.

By offering a collage of many different voices in this chapter, many from critical Black studies or from queer theory, I do not intend to syncretize them. They are not saying the same thing. They represent many schools of thought and different strategies. They are dissonant; they have tensions between them that I don't seek to resolve. They represent projects that in some cases also have dissonance with my own or might take issue with my invocation of them alongside my own. In these ways, the chapter mirrors the provisional assembly it seeks to encourage. Otherwise is not just one.

Our voices and bodies do not always converge for long. There is, as Minnesota poet Keno Evol writes, a kind of poly-fugitivity.[22] And yet the divergent comings together we assemble, and perhaps even the one I assemble with words here, can materialize otherwise possibilities.

I turn now to some of the possible textures of ecclesiology otherwise, derived from the sources drawn together in this dispatch. I gather textures we might notice in Christian assemblies that interrupt Christomodern violence. I

---

22  Keno Evol, "Poly-fugitivity: Utopian Relations in Dystopian Structures," Mn Artists, January 15, 2021, https://mnartists.walkerart.org/poly-fugitivity-utopian-relations-in -dystopian-structures.

note the embodied or incarnate, the fleshy; the improvised and indeed provisional; the apophatic and sometimes cataphatic; the coalitional and always plural; and finally, the sacramental.

## Embodied Assembly

Hardt and Negri write that "de- and remade, bodies resist. They have to resist in order to exist."[23] Bodily resistance is, again, at once personal and political. Production of subjectivity through resistance is central "not only to the subversion of the existing forms of power but also the constitution of alternative institutions of liberation."[24] As we practice assembly otherwise, we are about the business of both resisting coloniality and birthing (again and again) new personal and collective embodiments. This is resonant also with the enduring manifestation of Christian incarnation, an insistent birthing of holiness in flesh, the ongoing embodiment of God, of sacrality, of healing.

Hardt and Negri query the role of religion in these "alternative institutions of liberation" by commenting on a notable aspect of Foucault's writing from Iran when on commission from an Italian newspaper in 1978: "What we find most significant . . . is how he recognizes in the religious fundamentalism of the rebellion and its focus on bodies the elements of a biopolitical[25] power that, if deployed differently, diverted

---

23  Hardt and Negri, *Commonwealth*, 31.
24  Hardt and Negri, 31; see also x.
25  Note that Carter and Hardt and Negri use *biopolitical* differently. In Carter, it is an adjective for a characteristic of biopower: the biopolitical is a function of biopower. In Hardt

from its closure in the theocratic regime, could bring about a radical transformation of subjectivity and participate in a project of liberation."[26] In other words, while bodies and religion have merged to fuel modes of power over, there is other potency available to bodies "diverted" from theocratic closure. Hardt and Negri write that tapping this resistant potency will involve avoiding any bodily erasure through fundamentalisms, a stance which "refuses to let the bodies be eclipsed, and instead insists on their power."[27]

Assembly otherwise to empire is what Hardt and Negri describe as "plural social ontology."[28] This plural subjectivity arrives in ruptures and openings emerging from the multitude amid the oppressive power fields of modern empire, and they describe it as "always a queer event, a subversive process of subjectification that, shattering ruling identities and norms, reveals the link between power and freedom, and thereby inaugurates an alternative production of subjectivity."[29] While Hardt and Negri are not prescribing what Christian assembly otherwise could be, their language

---

and Negri, it's a description of resistance to biopower. Hardt and Negri use the term in juxtaposition to biopower: for them, biopolitics are the constructive and good potential of the commonwealth or multitude to resist biopower. This is confusing, and the confusion continues across several of the secondary articles I resource here, so throughout this text, I am avoiding use of the word *biopolitical* altogether. Under whatever terms, we are seeking to articulate power otherwise. I suppose it is appropriate to power otherwise that there will not just be one term for it, and sometimes our terms will contradict one another! I avoid unnecessary confusion here by dropping the term *biopolitical* in this book.

26  Hardt and Negri, 36.
27  Hardt and Negri, 38.
28  Michael Hardt and Antonio Negri, *Assembly* (Cambridge, MA: Belknap Press of Harvard University Press, 2009), 80.
29  Hardt and Negri, 62–63.

helps give it texture: opening, queer subversion that shatters the identities of coloniality, and certainly "plural social ontology."

Citing Judith Butler, they also speak to the precarity of all assembly otherwise to normative regimes. They highlight the ways that assembly, even the assembling of those most vulnerable to the regime's devastations, can respond to precarity "not by retreating behind the walls of identity but instead by constructing new, mobile constellations of shared life."[30] These constellations manage "to evade the fusional identitarian powers of control."[31] As we have seen, the churches have themselves been cartographers of these identitarian powers. Thus Christian assembly otherwise will need to practice other constellations of shared life; these will be deeply familiar to those Christians who have been practicing against empire for a long time and may be hard to recognize as Christian practice at all for others. Hardt and Negri offer a descriptive texture for the constellations of assembly otherwise, riffing on a transformation of Machiavelli's prince figure:

> A *new* Prince, though, will not be an individual or a central committee or a party. A Prince of the multitude is something like a chemical precipitate that already exists in suspension, dispersed throughout society, and under the right conditions, it will coalesce in solid form. It is also something like a musical

---

30  Hardt and Negri, 60.
31  Hardt and Negri, 60. Here they are speaking particularly of migration and poverty.

composition: the plural ontology of the multitude does not merge into one but instead the singularities (That is, the different social forces that continue to express their differences) discover harmonies and dissonances, common rhythms and syncopations. They compose a Prince. It is also something like the center of gravity of a dancing body.[32]

This royal subjectivity improvised in the common "creates a new gravitational field, a force of liberation."[33]

In this kind of productive assembly, Hardt and Negri write, the common always comes first and is driven by and expressive of "collective desire."[34] Hardt and Negri call this a "communitary anthropogenesis, which moves from the recognition of the ontology of the common to a project of its political affirmation."[35] Assembly is that by which we constitute otherwise; Hardt and Negri describe it, therefore, as a right, "a *constitutive* right." It is not a right that will be awarded by hegemonic power (and not a right that can be doled out by the church). It is a right insisted upon by the assembly, an emergent right, the right for "composing a social

---

32  Hardt and Negri, 228.

33  Hardt and Negri, 228.

34  Hardt and Negri, *Assembly*, 238. The common comes first; power comes second: "The common becomes, in the struggles, a joyful democratic passion something like a new natural right" (Hardt and Negri, Assembly, 238). Similarly, Carter describes how Foucault saw the need for "a politics of culture that seeks for ways to inhabit the radically democratizing possibilities of the global situation, but only by decoupling these possibilities from the new form of sovereignty (i.e., biopower) that seeks to own this terrain, the terrain of *bios* itself and in its totality, outright" (Carter, *Race*, 61). That sovereignty presides over racism; "democratizing possibilities" can interrupt it.

35  Hardt and Negri, *Assembly*, 238.

alternative, for taking power differently, through coopera-
tion and social production."[36]

I read here textures for Christian assembly otherwise: a
different center of gravity found in common, and one that
is midmotion, agile in dance. I imagine chemical elements
coming together, with rhythm and syncopation, composing
a sacramental solidity through our coalescence—or, as process theology would describe it, our concrescence. Ashon
Crawley describes something similar: "a performance that
is never about the one but about the plural, never about the
individual but about the social from which the individual
emerges . . . the various intensities of relationality not that
the music makes possible but that the vibration gathered as
sound and song makes evident as always already happening, the otherwise possibility in the flesh."[37] We comprise a
rhythmic sacramental body.

## Provisional Assembly

Lugones writes that "resistant subjectivity often expresses
itself infra-politically," where "infra-politics marks the turn
inward, in a politics of resistance, toward liberation. It shows
the power of communities of the oppressed in constituting
resistant meaning and each other against the constitution
of meaning and social organization by power." Again, we
hear the *constitutive* right. Because (thanks be!) "in our colonized, racially gendered, oppressed existences we are also

---

36  Hardt and Negri, 295.
37  Crawley, "Susceptibility," 23.

other than what the hegemon makes us be." And "that is an infra-political achievement."[38] The achievement is not once and for all; it is renewed and revised in a tense space.

This tension describes the heterotopography of any assembly otherwise; the tension is the momentum of the becoming-other. As Jordan writes, "Power must be conceived not as an assured possession or decisive victory but as a tense and always mutable field of relations."[39] And Lugones describes a kind of spring dynamic: "The relational subjective/intersubjective spring of liberation, as both adaptive and creatively oppositional." She repeatedly describes this dynamic or space as one of tension: "Resistance is the tension between subjectification (the forming/informing of the subject) and active subjectivity, that minimal sense of agency."[40] For Lugones, this is trespassing, playfulness, pilgrimage, travel "in the midst of people mindful to the tensions, desires, closures, cracks, and openings that make up the social."[41]

In his volume published just before this one in the *Dispatches* series, Ashley John Moyse explores the dehumanizing "malaise of the modern technological society" and stresses that Christian practice does not stop simply with gestures

---

38   María Lugones, *Pilgrimages/Peregrinajes: Theorizing Coalition against Multiple Oppressions* (Lanham, MD: Rowman & Littlefield, 2003), 746.

39   Jordan, *Convulsing*, 131.

40   Lugones also writes, "When I think of myself as a theorist of resistance, it is not because I think of resistance as the end or goal of political struggle, but rather as its beginning, its possibility" ("Decolonial," 746). She does not speak of a resistance sheerly for resistance's sake. She will also say, "The intent is not to glorify resistance to oppressions, but rather to understand resistance as adumbrating our possibilities" (*Pilgrimages/Peregrinajes*, 37).

41   Lugones, *Pilgrimages/Peregrinajes*, 11.

of dissent against this culture of dissatisfaction.[42] Dissent involves ongoing practice and formation: "Dissent is to be regarded a material social performance, an art where discernment and protest are practiced to expose and rebuke fallen powers and principalities such that human life might be nurtured and fulfillment of all life might be actualized. The target of such dissent is not the innate conditions of existence, but rather in what humans have invented—or imagined and brought to bear."[43] This practice of dissent from the dehumanization of the modern technological project can be a kind of Christian discipleship of dissent, and it is, as I have been exploring here of assembly otherwise, ongoing. It is not a once-and-done, "spontaneous fiat."[44] Similar to the way I am envisioning improvisational practices that are themselves provisional, the way of Jesus imaged by Moyse requires cultivation. Yet importantly, for neither of our visions does this entail perpetual dissatisfaction, which would only feed the systems we seek to resist. To the contrary, these practices of dissent can practice satisfaction and the cultivation of an ability to be what adrienne maree brown, remembering Audre Lorde's legacy, describes as "satisfiable selves."[45] Practices of incarnation as humans, humanizing practice, can be savory and sacrament.

Such Christian practice otherwise can "people" a space previously rendered inhuman, much as Lugones speaks of

---

42 Ashley John Moyse, *The Art of Living for a Technological Age: Toward a Humanizing Performance* (Minneapolis: Fortress, 2021), 129 and 140.
43 Moyse, 138.
44 Moyse, 141.
45 adrienne maree brown, *Pleasure Activism: The Politics of Feeling Good* (Chico, CA: AK, 2019).

the "peopled ground" of the "project of decoloniality." I am searching for Christian practices that provisionally constitute resistant meaning. More than searching, I am readying my own embodiment for them, in any moment. I wish to encourage the same for Christian ecclesiology. Disrupting long-standing oppressions of Christian colonial hegemony requires new agilities to do otherwise. This is an embodied agility and readiness, on both personalized and ecclesial levels, for "taking up the nonscripted possibilities in the cracks in domination," as Lugones writes, "in the spirit of disruption." These possibilities are ongoing, provisional, improvised. This is a very fluid, very unscripted invitation to Christian assembling, which I am imagining as sometimes possible in what Lugones describes as the "tense inhabitation of the colonial difference" and "the tension of the colonial wound."[46]

That inhabitation is never assured and comes to birth in precarity. As my teacher Otto Maduro wrote of resistant ways of knowing, "The paradox of a way of knowing that aims to undermine an authoritarian, hierarchical, exploitive social system is that, in order not to mimic, legitimate, and serve as an instrument of that very system, it needs to shape itself as an open, humble, dialogical, consistently self-examining way of understanding and producing knowledge, even more liable to be destroyed by the very social system it emerges against."[47] What Maduro describes of epistemological practice is also true of other resistant practices:

---

46  Lugones, *Pilgrimages/Peregrinajes*, 746–50.
47  Otto Maduro, "An(other) Invitation to Epistemological Humility: Notes towards a Self-Critical Approach to Counter-Knowledges," in *Decolonizing Epistemologies: Latina/o*

open, humble, dialogical, vulnerable, or as Crawley names it, "susceptible."[48]

This can appear extremely precarious or, as Lugones writes, "like a very attenuated sense of agency," for it is a "variegated, dominated, in resistance to a variety of inter-meshed and interlocking oppressions, aggregate that pulls in different ways, sometimes in unison, but more often in many directions, dispersed but 'intent,' in a loose sense of intentionality, on overcoming social fragmentation, the purity of language, disembodiment, a unilinear history, mythical attachments to place or communities of the same."[49] It is up to very good work but will often not be recognized as such. Christian assembly otherwise will be susceptible, vulnerable, precarious—not just in the short term but as its character-istic terms.

For Jordan, the otherwise has the aesthetics of camp or drag: "The inhabitation is always incomplete; the perfor-mances, refracted and anticipatory."[50] And so we ready our-selves for Christian practice that, like the aesthetics of camp, "abandons the ruses of continuity for the display of discon-tinuity." (This will be a drastic change for some Christians.) We ready for "surprising juxtaposition or constellation."[51]

---

*Theology and Philosophy*, ed. Ada Maria Isasi-Diaz and Eduardo Mendieta (New York: Fordham University Press, 2012), 102.

48  Crawley, "Susceptibility," 11–38.

49  Lugones, *Pilgrimages/Peregrinajes*.

50  Jordan, "Return," 53. He writes, "They are closer to camp or drag than to perfect con-formity or accomplished identity. But for that very reason they resist the regime of iden-tities proposed by sexuality as its starting point" (53).

51  Mark D. Jordan, "Notes on Camp Theology," in *Dancing Theology in Fetish Boots*, ed. Lisa Isherwood and Mark D. Jordan (London: SCM, 2010), 183. He also points to the "col-lage, montage, the splice or jump" (183).

And this refracted, spliced practice will be at once "both apophatic theology and an incarnational theology."[52]

## Apophatic Assembly

There is something both apophatic and cataphatic about assembly otherwise, as though it slips both under and over the frequency of empire's radars, under and beyond the frequencies of bodily alignment into which coloniality has trained us.

Looking for speech apart from those frequencies, Jordan wonders "whether some Christian speech might still afford other possibilities for contesting the regime of sexuality," such that Christian words might yet "disrupt the regime rather than copy it and reinforce it." We have seen that Christian powers are adept at copying and reinforcing hegemony, but Jordan asks, "Could the return of another Christianity offer an alternative idiom in which to articulate bodies and pleasures without endorsing the reign of King Sex?"[53]

Foucault diagnoses a challenge here, in that in modernity we confess the self without renunciation of the self.[54] Thus though we may want that "alternative idiom" described by Jordan, we easily endorse the reign of sexuality as we reinscribe ourselves again and again with no mysterious surplus beyond our understanding in which to fall. Rather

---

52  Jordan, 189. It will also be enough to get Marcella pulling on her dancing boots in the beyond. As Jordan writes of Marcella Althaus-Reid, "An indecent theology, she says, requires mismatches. It imagines rupture" (184).

53  Jordan, "Return," 41. Similarly, he writes in his *Ethics of Sex* of the helpful nature of negative theology (153).

54  See Foucault et al., *Technologies*.

we, through self-maintenance, repeatedly bolster hegemonic constructions of how things are in King Sex's court.

Foucault writes in some of his later lectures that there remains a possibility of undoing the technologies of the self. As Jordan summarizes, "The modern self is the epistemological Christian self without the paradox of sacrifice, which has been replaced by governmental management," and thus subjectivity otherwise "requires two motions: undoing the modern machinery, then evading what Foucault takes to be the Christian paradoxes of sacrifice."[55] It is as though the apophasis at play in nonmodern self-renunciation undoes the sturdy container of individuality without which we become solid units of biopower or its dehumanized other. A spoonful of apophasis seems good for the soul!

Similarly, Jordan argues that the modern regime differs from its Christian parentage—not in being un-Christian, for it is still incestuously sister and child to Christianity, as we have seen of Christomodernity but in that it no longer has the theological reserves that once underwrote or unwrote the self. The problematic result is that "there is no longer a hidden silence . . . no negative ideal."[56] As an example, Jordan looks particularly at Jesus's silence on sex and the restructuring of social relations as agape community and then Paul's struggle with "the ideal of a life beyond sex." These now curious early markers of body and pleasure in the early Jesus movement point to what Jordan names theologically helpful

---

55  Jordan, *Convulsing*, 140. In my *Power For*, I have explored how the Christian theme of sacrifice might offer rich ground for the production of subjectivity, not sheerly its abnegation.

56  Jordan, "Return," 50.

"ancient reserves."[57] Another example would be the ancient "Christian case against marriage" explored by Dale Martin (as mentioned in chapter 1).

Jordan summarizes the way in which apophasis gets compressed out of Christomodernity: "When the libraries of Christian speech are rewritten into the modern regimes of 'secularized' sexuality . . . when Christian pastoral discourses pass over into sexuality properly speaking, the ancient reserves, the principles of negation, do *not* pass with them."[58]

Jordan determines that "once Christian speeches capitulate to sexuality in this way, the ancient reserve is indeed undone and Christian chatter about sex no longer deserves to be called Christian *theology*." Jordan's diagnosis is precise: "Christian chatter about sex becomes a local *dialect* within the regime of sexuality. It serves as another courtier to King Sex."[59] Instead, Jordan urges us to recall a "disruptive silence," a negative theology, an apophasis.[60] In "acknowledging the reserves of silence, one acknowledges as well the limits on embodied performance, and so resists the regime of sexuality at its starting point." The practices of bodies in

---

57  Jordan, 49. Jordan also notes that "much does pass. . . . But the most significant difference is not salient because it is a generalized absence—the lack of theological reserve, the erasure of Jesus' marked silence" (50).

58  Jordan, 49–50. However, the reserves are still there to be invoked: "These ancient reserves in Christian speech about sex survive as limiting negations underneath the enormous elaboration of pastoral discourses. They qualify or rebuke the endless loquacity about Christians' sexual activity. . . . The reserves are principles of negation that can be invoked unexpectedly to undo the assurance of sexual categories or rules in such texts" (49).

59  Jordan, 51.

60  Jordan, 52, in strong resonance to his work in *Ethics of Sex* on negative theology.

coalition will always be provisional, enjoying a theologizing "more accomplished in syncopation and silence, in parody and avowal, than in diagnostic certainties and political programs."[61]

Those "ancient reserves" do still linger outside the courts of power, another peopled ground of odd Bible characters and saints, "sacramental characters of an outmoded Christianity,"[62] still available to visit our tense inhabitations of colonial difference and enrich the plural ontologies we embody there. Calling them in, we remember apophasis, or we slip perhaps in cataphasis, a crowd of noisy saints.

In contrast, the modern confession of the self, like the fall without a Genesis story world around it, throws oneself repeatedly up against the boundaries of the self's individualized container, thus callousing and strengthening the constructed boundaries of the self: I am doing my work, my growth, I am coming into myself through this therapeutic confession of who I am. This reifies identity rather than realizing coalition and plural ontology.

The nonmodern confession of self can access expanse and plentitude in a way that the modern contortion of it will not. The resistance exercise against this boundary claims the expanse again and insists on the plenty, in part through coalition. Coalition engages plentitude in heightening the obviousness of otherness and difference, in maintaining that

---

61  Jordan, "Return," 53.
62  Jordan, 50. Jordan explores how characters, whether from the Bible or hagiography, offer a "complex temporality that cannot be captured by any identity." Poised as they are between "citation to scriptural past and by anticipation of a divinely fixed eternity," they are not therefore "a measurable or manageable unit of bio-power" (52).

tension while working together, in feeling sometimes conflicting feelings in that space, and in existing as actual bodies there, different and together. In coalition, we feel our way into "subjectivity," into a larger sense of world and being, both communal and uniquely personalized.

As people do the modern ethics of sexuality without the softening of a theological, spiritual reserve (both in the West broadly speaking and also in the churches), sexuality has become a literalism; it is flat, it becomes a program of what our bodies must be about. And we also have ended up with a less susceptible, positive notion of subjectivity, unrenounced; it is similarly flat, essential to "who you are," not a negotiable mystery, and far from a plural social ontology! Meanwhile, due to the interiorizing technology of Christomodernity, both one's spirituality and one's sexuality are inside the "self" somewhere, personally hidden and yet operative in creating public coloniality. And for those not on the "light" side of coloniality, all these problematic categories (the inner, your sexuality, woman, man, human) are at best on loan from the white hegemon, terms with which to do a commerce of intelligibility for survival's sake.

Carter also articulates a need for a kind of apophatic hold on Christian knowing and practice. Whiteness involves a "disposition of possession or attachment"—a disposition undone by cataphatic multiplicity and the apophasis it invokes. In Carter's words, "It is precisely the disposition of possession or attachment, rather than dispossession or ascetic detachment, that lies behind the pseudotheological disposition of whiteness and the violent divisions that have come to mark human existence as the outworking of this division."[63] Apophasis refuses the possessive grip.

This "ascetic detachment" calls to mind Foucault's list of counter practices possible within the Christian pastorate. Apophasis and cataphasis are counterconfession; they back away from or exceed the confession of self itself taught by the hegemonic pastorate.

We need to reengage the tension of limits, relearning apophasis, which I argue that we can do through multiplicity. The multiple does, perhaps paradoxically, invoke the silence of mystery. The cacophany of the multiple and the occasions in which it coalesces into complex harmonic beauty can invoke an awestruck apophatic response.

Jordan writes that, after remembering silence, speech about sex (and I think we can extend this to theologizing as a whole) "might take up dozens of genres—of inquiry, parable, exhortation, invocation, benediction—but each of them would leave the erotic open to refract a past it must revere without repeating and to anticipate a future it must await without picturing."[64] Always dozens, always multiple. As Lugones will claim, "I want to mark the need to keep a multiple reading of the resistant self in relation."[65]

Cataphasis is the apophatic other to imperial identity. Cataphasis is the sound of multiplicity; it invokes our apophasis rather than our identitarian confession. Apophasis falls under and cataphasis in surplus beyond identitarian

---

63  Carter, *Race*, 353.
64  Jordan, "Return," 53.
65  Lugones, "Decolonial," 748.

control: both help maintain the tense edges of sacramental heterotopography. Theologizing otherwise practices the apophatic and cataphatic expansions of the multiple.

## Coalitional Assembly

As Hardt and Negri write, "A key scene of political action today, seen from this vantage point, involves the struggle over the control or autonomy of the production of subjectivity. The multitude makes itself by composing in the common the singular subjectivities that result from this process."[66] This is a reorientation of subjectivity. Not an interior individuality, but one that is singular, articulated, and touched in the common, felt into shape, however temporary.

For Lugones, resistance involves "a coalitional starting point." This is where we learn about one another: "In thinking of the starting point as coalitional because the fractured locus is in common, the histories of resistance at the colonial difference are where we need to dwell, learning about each other."[67] Learning about one another, not just focusing on the oppressor we resist, enables "a furthering of the logic of difference and multiplicity."[68] This is also to say, "Communities rather than individuals enable the doing; one does with someone else, not in individualist isolation."[69]

---

66 Hardt and Negri, *Commonwealth*, x.
67 Lugones, "Decolonial," 753.
68 Lugones, 755.
69 Lugones, 754. She similarly writes in "Heterosexualism" that "we perform a transformation of communal relations" (189).

Assembly otherwise is therefore just that: it is an assembling, not a solo Christian practice. This is a contrast to Christomodernity's interiorizing pressures and navel gazing pieties. Christian assembling gathers amid multitude.[70] The multitude is a making, not a stagnant or even consistent being. It is horizontally constituted multiplicity, dark and queer. We have been so accustomed to hierarchically constituted church. This is one of the deadening travesties of coloniality. When we shift into agency and momentum as Christian assembly amid multitude, we will probably not, at least at first, recognize Christian polity as such (meanwhile, these Christian embodiments are already at play in forms both recognized and largely unrecognized).

Assembly amid multitude will need malleable and responsive ecclesial structures. We'll need ways of recognizing Spirit-filled authority on local and provisional levels. We'll need to expect seemingly extreme difference and discord over how Christian assembly works. A challenge will be to nonetheless recognize one another as members of a cross-locality, a constitutive, living body of Christ. While it may appear a dissolute ecclesiology, Christian assembly in the multitude does not diminish the body of Christ, a body that was, from its conception, open, wounded, dripping, transgressive, unbounded, given away. In this sense, assembly

---

70 Joerg Rieger and Kwok Pui-lan explore a theology of the multitude in conversation with the Occupy Movement. In their discussion of "multitude," they compellingly work with both Korean *minjung* theology and Hardt and Negri. I resonate with many of their emphases but choose a more diffuse language for Christian presence in multitude: I will tend to say not "church of the multitude" but "Christian assembly amid multitude." See Joerg Rieger and Pui-lan Kwok, *Occupy Religion: Theology of the Multitude*, Religion in the Modern World (Lanham, MD: Rowman & Littlefield, 2012).

amid multitude is true to form and as uncapturable and impossible to rubricate as God's embodiment ever was.

The hegemon disrupts bonds; resistance weaves them, insists on them. This weaving must be regularly practiced; multiplicity has to be maintained in the tense space that would close it down. Thus Lugones writes that in resistance to coloniality, "the emphasis is on maintaining multiplicity at the point of reduction"—the reductions of humanity, the foreclosure of difference. Those insisting on maintaining a multiplicity refuse the colonial logic, the logic of oppression, for "among the logics at work are the many logics meeting the logic of oppression: many colonial differences, but one logic of oppression." The many colonial differences have a "logic of coalition" that is "defiant of the logic of dichotomies," since dichotomies are another reiteration of the one, as "differences are never seen in dichotomous terms."[71]

When Christian assembly embodies logics of coalition, it moves apart from and against the logics of oneness it has known so well. It sheds dichotomies. It moves until Christian practice becomes a thing beyond white womanhood. Until it becomes a variable assembly of dark practices that no one can embody as a woman or a man. Until it is not finally something we can call "church" or theology, because those have been units of the logic of oppression.

Robyn Henderson-Espinoza writes of the way the recognition of difference, while indecent to the logics of oppression, remains essential. While "it is on all accounts an indecent and (un)virtuous act to recognizes difference(s),"

---

71  Lugones, "Decolonial," 755.

it is precisely that vital "perversion" that opens the way to creativity. As Henderson-Espinoza writes, the indecent recognition of differences "marks a new creative opening for bodies to materialize on a plane of becoming."[72] Coalescing differences mark creative wellsprings.

## Sacramental Assembly

To return again to Lugones's colonial/modern gender system, heterogender is the brick and mortar of racialized oppression in that system. Whiteness is constituted by white man and white woman, and their relationship is not reciprocal: whiteness is constituted by men and the women who reproduce them. Lugones's approach makes clear that gender applies only to the "light" side, to colonial whiteness, and humanity applies only to this light side. All else in this framework is animal, nonhuman. Coloniality constructs no man or woman who is not white and in the heterosex binary. There are no women of color, no men of color. There are no queer men, and no queer women. But this dehumanizing is often not named, and the extent of its impact not recognized, such that in work for equity, people will think to solve problems with a mission such as "We need rights for more men and women—those of color and those queer." The work is futile and often violent, despite good intention, because there is no actual space in the Christomodern frame for other bodies or for a radical sacramental peopling. This

---

72 Robyn Henderson-Espinoza, "Perversion, Ethics, and Creative Disregard: Indecency as the Virtue to Ethical Perversion," in *Indecent Theologians: Marcella Althaus-Reid and the Next Generation of Postcolonial Activists*, ed. Nicolas Panotto (Alameda, CA: Borderless, 2016), 230.

is also how inclusion work can proceed in the church, prob-lematically. It can, through more inclusion in a colonial system, seek to bolster control of the standing hierarchies rather than participating in the rebirth of holy humanities.

In the tense fissures of colonial difference and even when greatly challenged by oppressions, queer and dark beauty, power, and care persistently glisten. While many have been practicing Christian faith and improvising Spirit amid queerness and darkness for a long time, "theology" has been owned by the same colonial power domain that creates whiteness and the "light" side. Church and theology have been major players in "racialized, ableist heterocapital," to return to Gumbs's phrase. Queer, dark Christian practices arise at the fractured site of colonial difference. They are not "other" theologies, as though they could be the acceptable alternative ordained or approved by the colonizer. In terms of coloniality, "other" theologies that theology accepted into the mainstream guild as authorized marginalized perspec-tives are only "theologies" in the same sense that we can pretend there are nonwhite women. In Lugones's frame for coloniality, the woman is always and only a white category, and in this sense, we can say that theology in the West is also a white colonial discourse. Acknowledging theology elsewhere (falsely so) is too easily only lip service; it may not disrupt the colonizing order.[73]

---

73  Althaus-Reid writes so vividly about the limits of liberation theology in this way. See her *Indecent Theology: Theological Perversions in Sex, Gender, and Politics* (London: Routledge, 2000) or her "From Liberation Theology to Indecent Theology: The Trouble with Normality in Theology," in *Latin American Liberation Theology: The Next Generation*, ed. Ivan Petrella (Maryknoll, NY: Orbis, 2005). Also see the essays in her honor in *Dancing Theology in Fetish*

As Lugones explains, resistant responses disappear when absorbed by hegemonic systems: "If we only weave man and woman into the very fabric that constitutes the self in relation to resisting, we erase the resistance itself."[74] Similarly, "theology" and "church" too easily erase resistance and reify coloniality. All that can travel to the site of colonial difference—all that was already there of this faith all along—are loose Christian practices, mobile and provisional.

The category of church itself now adheres too cleanly to a system of biopower to function as church in modes of resistance against and within it. Even Foucault, as Jordan writes, "draws the startling conclusion that Christianity understood as church, as an organization of pastoral power is *not* ascetical, communal, mystical, scriptural, or eschatological"[75]—that is, it is not any of its own forms of counter conduct.

It becomes clear that we cannot transfer hegemonic categories onto the nonhegemonic and expect to achieve equity or inclusion. It will only achieve a deeper cloak for hegemony. Hegemonic terms do not travel out of hegemony; they simply expand and disseminate hegemony, even if it seems to be a lending of terms or a "sharing" of power.

---

*Boots*, ed. Lisa Isherwood and Mark D. Jordan (London: SCM, 2010), several of which address this topic directly.

74  Lugones, "Decolonial," 749. On this point, Cocks and Houlbrook summarize Joan Scott's point that lifting up the voices of the marginalized can have the effect of masking the process of their marginalization. This can set or fix in place the marginality itself. Thus Scott "calls for us to try and understand how categories like marginal/central, normal/abnormal are made in the first place, and also how these ideas are policed and enforced" (Cocks and Houlbrook, *Modern History of Sexuality*, 6, on Joan Scott, "The Evidence of Experience," in *The Gay and Lesbian Studies Reader* [London: Routledge, 1993]).

75  Jordan, *Convulsing*, 131.

Hegemony doesn't share, and the master's tools won't dismantle the master's house.

Thus, Lugones will conclude, "Our possibilities lie in communality rather than subordination; they do not lie in parity with our superior in the hierarchy that constitutes the coloniality."[76] And Althaus-Reid will warn that "what we can call the Queer difference disappears when it asserts its own sexual rights in accordance with the heterosexual system."[77]

Thus we are not practicing marginal theologies or doing theology from the spaces of the colonized. We are not doing church at the margins or even church against empire. Christian practice at the site of the colonial difference invokes a differing holiness, marked bestial and profane by coloniality.

Recognizing that theology as such cannot continue into the dark spaces crushed by a pseudotheological modernity, Carter advocates and himself demonstrates a dispositional shift for theology.[78] Without such a shift, theological discourse as it has developed in the modern West remains contained by the construct of white supremacy and is thus trapped in distortion as pseudotheology. He provides an example of how Christians might assemble otherwise: his vision is of "a lived or performed theology that seeks to resist modernity's pseudotheological pretensions through its instantiation or embodiment of a mode of sociopolitical

---

76  Lugones, "Decolonial," 752.
77  Althaus-Reid, *Queer God*, 123.
78  Carter, *Race*, 374.

existence that orients itself" from what Carter terms the "Christ form," in contrast to "the modern nation form."[79]

In developing this "Christ form," Carter refocuses Christians on Jesus's particular body. Incarnation will mean what should have been obvious: a body for Jesus. Christ's body cannot continue to be abstracted as church and theology have done in creating a theological supremacy system. To return to Jesus's flesh, Carter lifts up sources from Black American literature that "moved to theologically overcome the modern problem of race" and did so "precisely in moving in the direction of envisioning Jesus as the Christ and Christ's flesh as Jewish covenantal flesh and not racial-colonial flesh."[80]

Jesus, Jesus as a human and a body, was situated as both a Jew under empire and a creature in relationship to the Creator. I notice how far that body is from the only full body in the colonial/modern gender system, the white "man." Jesus is not a person in the colonial/modern gender system, which is precisely why remembering Jesus's body, and practice in remembrance of that body, resists coloniality.

Jordan also notes how trapped our ideas of Jesus will become under the hegemony of modern sexuality: "There is no outside, not even for Jesus. If Jesus *could* stand outside, the whole regime would be called into question by his

---

79  Carter, 52.
80  Carter, 7. Carter envisions "the particularity of Christ's flesh—which is Jewish covenantal flesh and not Jewish racial flesh . . . as the material horizon within which creation is ordered toward the God of Abraham" (Carter, 7).

displacement, his refusal to enter the dichotomy between heterosexual and homosexual."[81]

I imagine that Christian assembly otherwise can invoke such an outside for Jesus; it is a practiced heterotopy. As Carter describes it, "Christ's flesh, which is Jewish covenantal flesh, is a *taxis*, a material arrangement of freedom that discloses the historical transcendence of God."[82] Christian assembly in the tension of the colonial difference practices that "material arrangement of freedom"; it is incarnational practice. It is constituted by assembled bodies, and it constitutes actual covenantal body of Christ.

Diagnosing just how far the field of theology has come from the flesh of Jesus, Carter tells theology that it must have "a new modality."[83] Theology is currently built on a kind of vast disembodiment: "The aesthetic imagination of the modern intellectual is conditioned on obfuscating the real world of pain and cultural trauma as the condition of thought."[84] Instead, Carter points to bodies: Theology "must do its work in company with and out of the disposition of those facing death, those with the barrel of a shotgun to their backs, for this is the disposition of the crucified Christ, who is the revelation of the triune God."

Tragically, however, "it is just such a vision of that theology, functioning as racial discourse and in the intellectual

---

81  Jordan, "Return," 51. He writes, "Under the regime of sexuality, everyone should have a sexual identity at the end of a proper sexual development—whether they remain celibate or not" (Jordan, "Return," 51).

82  Carter, *Race*, 8.

83  Carter, 377.

84  Carter, 376.

modality of whiteness, has foreclosed."[85] As such, as a racial discourse, as a cartographer of the colonial/modern gender system, the disciplining church and its discipline of theology have also been constraining the ongoing incarnation of God. Thus Althaus-Reid writes evocatively of the need for queer lovers to beckon God out of the closet.[86] This is because God's own possibilities for becoming are diminished by Christo-modern distortions. God as revealed in Christ emerges as fragile but resilient embodiment. While James Cone writes of Christ in the Black ghetto,[87] and Althaus-Reid writes of the rosary tucked lovingly in the trouser pocket at the salsa bar,[88] foundationally white, heterosexist Christomodern theology not only misses its point amid its pseudotheological distraction but further loads the guns pointed at the ghetto and the bar. King Sex distracts us with endless ecclesial fights over sexuality, and while backs are turned, divinity is in a stranglehold alongside God's beloved. The work of King Sex is a disciplinary function of the light side. The light side is hallowed by the church, and theology is one of its disci-plines. In contrast, the indecency of dark and queer sex and the crises of life and death navigated daily by dark and queer bodies point the way to assembly otherwise.

Lugones writes, "What I am proposing in working toward a decolonial feminism is to learn about each other as resisters to the coloniality of gender at the colonial

---

85  Carter, 377.
86  Althaus-Reid, *Indecent Theology*, 69; Althaus-Reid, *Queer God*, 2, 54, 143, 158.
87  James Cone, *Black Theology and Black Power*, 50th anniversary ed. (Maryknoll, NY: Orbis, 2018).
88  Althaus-Reid, *Queer God*, 4.

difference, without necessarily being an insider to the worlds of meaning from which resistance to the coloniality arises."[89] This gives the cue that Christian assembly otherwise cannot rely on being an insider to the worlds of meaning we have known as "theology" and "church." "Theology" (like all the categories of the light side, like "men" and "women") doesn't survive the transit into dark and queer. Nor does "church." What remains are practices, collectively improvised, shifting.

Carter, working with Maximus the Confessor's Christology, writes of the ways in which humanity is restored in Christ: "Human identity as Christ has instantiated it can be called an intrahuman identity."[90] Human beings receive themselves from other human beings, and in that reciprocity also receive God: "For in receiving oneself from one another—that is, in subsisting in another on the basis of shared humanity and thus on the basis of a shared, non-idolatrous status as creature in relationship to the Creator—one in fact receives God and thereby is most fully oneself."[91]

In this intrahuman reception, we people the ground of nonmodern life potential. Here Christ's own flesh enables a birth of new embodiment apart from the flesh either suffocated or striated by empire. It is not the only way counter flesh happens against Christomodernity; it is one way and invokes the body of a particular Jew whose body was erased by empire. Insistent reincarnation of the holy where dominating powers have denied humanity is Christianity's oldest

89  Lugones, "Decolonial," 753.
90  Carter, *Race*, 353.
91  Carter, 353.

story to offer. That sacramental reincarnation is our practice otherwise.

By now, coloniality has deeply contorted what many perceive and experience the sacred to be. Yet, with a fierce persistence, often shamed by hegemonic powers if not entirely off the radar of the hegemon, sacrament emerges on coloniality's unpeopled ground, a sacred ebullience midwifed by Black, brown, or queer vivacity, and more.

Beholding this sacramental ebullience, the churches (including those that are Black led, women led, or queer led) can legislate and shame it, and in so doing continue coloniality. We can embrace but on predetermined, conditional terms, and in so doing continue coloniality. Or we can, without claims to ownership or even full understanding, boost and celebrate the persistent ebullient incarnation of holiness on this earth. We can sometimes join its songs. We can regard the radical interruption of sacramental life and follow its lead.

Longing for such an interruption, Althaus-Reid determines that "what the Eucharist lacks . . . is the symbolics of the exchange and the transgression of an order."[92] Likewise, Jordan emphasizes the radicality of sacrament: "The sacraments are, on some theological accounts, means of participation in the ritual power of Jesus. This is a power to perform new selves."[93]

What then is sacrament in the tension of the colonial difference? The new selves performed cannot be a reification

---

92  Althaus-Reid, *Queer God*, 122.
93  Jordan, "Return," 53.

of the identity strictures of dominative power over/through. Rather, sacrament incarnates a peopled ground on the contours of the earth that have been designated inhabitable. As Cláudio Carvalhaes guides us, "We must realize our deep connections with all from the lower classes, all the poor—in whatever religion or color they come—and expand this solidarity to include animals, rivers, oceans, birds, and the whole earth. Only through that confluence of mutualities and belonging does our prayer become God's breath in the world."[94]

In searching for "how to think about intimate, everyday resistant interactions to the colonial difference,"[95] Lugones gives language we can borrow for imagining sacrament in the tense opening amid the colonial difference. Can we experiment with spiritual practices that are "intimate, everyday resistant interactions"? Can we taste the joy of chrism in the fissures?

We cannot do so as "church" or even as "theology"; those categories stay with the hegemon. Like gender, they do not travel. But there is manifold space, indeed the potential for innumerable heterotopies, for plural improvisational practices, for Christian assembly, for the spill of chrism, for embodiments of christic becoming-other.

Lugones sees that the forcible pressure of coloniality "is met in the flesh over and over by oppositional responses grounded in a long history of oppositional responses and

---

94 Cláudio Carvalhaes, *Liturgies from Below: Praying with People at the Ends of the Earth* (Nashville: Abingdon, 2020), 4. Also see Cláudio Carvalhaes, *Praying with Every Heart: Orienting Our Lives to the Wholeness of the World* (Eugene, OR: Cascade, 2021).

95 Lugones, "Decolonial," 743.

lived as sensical in alternative, resistant socialities at the colonial difference." I urge us to practice sacrament as such, as "movement toward coalition that impels us to know each other as selves that are thick, in relation, in alternative soci-alities, and grounded in tense, creative inhabitations of the colonial difference."[96]

Let us know one another as selves that are thick, queer, and dark. Let us taste the presence of holiness in alternative sociality that may not be intelligible from the balconies or altars of the hegemon; indeed, they likely appear heretical and indecent.

We assemble sacrament: in the flesh, pressing against the tense distinctions of colonial othering. We assemble sac-rament: the infrapolitical lived as sensible, tactile, savory, studded with inclusions of the holy. We assemble sacrament: plural social divine ontology that we can taste and see.

We cannot claim "the church as a resistant sociality," like we cannot say that "women" enact oppositional responses. We are here only as the peopled ground of alternative sociality—not the master's tools, not the hegemon's cate-gories, not the hegemon's subjectivities, not, finally, the hegemon's subjects. Our assemblies are of bodies, skin, plea-sure, marked by chrism, and as such, Christian.

There is no room in modern Western pseudotheology for the quotidian pain and christological revelation of dark flesh nor for the pain and incarnational possibilities of queer love. But there is room otherwise; dark bodies and queer sex interrupt the space and time of coloniality. The interruption

---

96   Lugones, 748.

comes not from dark bodies passively but from the joy and pleasure and assembled power of dark bodies. The interruption comes not from queer bodies only—perhaps made simulacrums of straight, white, monied couples—but from the transgressive sex decent theology will not acknowledge, from the indecency of queerness, the promiscuity and fundamental disruption of queerness. The interruption to the Christomodern domain is not made by the inclusion of dark or queer identity, identities that can fit neatly under coloniality because they stay in their place. The interruption is one of dark and queer practice. We assemble otherwise in queer and dark Christian practice. Here we say, "the body of Christ," and we mean it, in all its humanizing and deifying potential.

There are many ways to resist biopower. There need to be many ways, not all of them Christian. It is important that some of them not be Christian; it is a Christian hegemony we are resisting. Yet there is a unique contour to Christian resistance. Contrary to the cellular control of biopower, counter to a system that erases souls and bodies, the sacramental face-to-face encounter of "body" given "for you" offers unique potency. Against Christomodern biopower, Christian practice has a body to offer otherwise.

In the kairotic space of colonial difference, no longer as church, Christians assemble otherwise than the Christomodern embodiments to which they have been conditioned, feeling the tension in the different musculature of resistance. With the attention to full presence with one another that artistic improvisation always requires, we practice the embodiment of a divine body given over for redistribution among the profaned so that the profaned might become the righteousness of God.

Christian assembly needs to be, should have always been, a cultivating ground for depth of feeling,[97] for embodied and yes erotic knowing, for the savor of life, for the taste of something like the fatness and libation of the mountain in Isaiah 25. It should be one of the places where we learn what satisfaction tastes like. Where we learn to navigate as satisfiable selves.[98] Where we practice a yes to life from a very young and a very old age.

Christian assembly can come together in the tense matrices in which we are fundamentally dissatisfied with the negation of coloniality, as we are practicing differing satisfactions. The pleasures and satiety of sacramental assembly throw into sharp relief the negating, numbing powers of racialized, ableist heterocapital. We cocreate and realize pleasure and power that unravels negation and actively resists it. And the names for these practices are old and familiar: communion, absolution, baptism.

If Eucharist is not a thanksgiving of embodied yes, what is it? If the sacraments are not forming us as a body collective that feels life and insists upon it ever more widely, what are they doing?

Sacramental practice is repeated, ordinary, habitual. Christians cannot (in any future I can now foresee) stop actively practicing decolonization if we are to stay the momentum of imperial tendencies so deeply engrained in our

---

97  See Audre Lorde, "Uses of the Erotic: The Erotic as Power," in *Sister Outsider: Essays and Speeches*, 41–48 (Berkeley, CA: Crossing, 1984); and Brock, *Journeys by Heart*.

98  brown, *Pleasure Activism*.

previous embodiments as church. Sacramental practice strengthens our ability to improvise the creative wellsprings of life that christic bodies are here in the world to tend and beautify.

Despite my enthusiasm for this sacramental practice, I am not suggesting that Christian people are fundamental inventors of the otherwise. The otherwise is plural; its pluralities already exist, and it can spring from multiple origins. At the same time, Christian people, resisting the dominating technologies familiar to church and theology, can (and have) embody the otherwise. And they can add their offerings of festival and sanctity there.

The otherwise both does and does not need inventing. The otherwise is a past reality and also a future. It does not need inventing in this sense: it is not the church's next project or next colonial mission. And it does not need inventing in this sense: it is already invented, already manifoldly innovated. In all forms I can imagine to list—practical, theoretical, academic, grassroots, sensual, literary, artistic—the otherwise to Christomodernity already breathes and has been breathing. There are rich examples. In literature and art alone, one could savor years of exploration of the otherwise.

There are so many manifestations of the otherwise that in offering any examples in print, I risk narrowing the scope of plentitude and making the otherwise seem more particular than it is. (It is always particular to a time and place and the materiality there, to particular bodies and creatures, but that particularity is never predetermined or limited—*your* particulars work too.) Nonetheless, here are three examples that have beckoned to me in my own particularity, three invitations to the otherwise from ancestors to whom I listen: James Cone riffs with spirituals and jazz.[99] Marcela Althaus-Reid beckons toward a journey to your local gay bar with a rosary in your pocket.[100] And whales! They beckon too. Alexis Pauline Gumbs intuits how those ancestors, swimming alongside the death ships of the Middle Passage, held out the knowing of a breath otherwise to the suffocating passengers in the holds of the Middle Passage. The whales always knew another way to breathe, and the otherwise is always swimming just alongside coloniality's death grip.[101]

The manifold otherwise is already breathing, even in a breath-stealing world trapped under the leg of police and the necropolitics of respiratory pandemic response. Thus, church people, the otherwise is not a thing you need invent. It is improvisational life against the momentum of the embodied imperialism that the church has become and against the imperialism that our own bodies have come to incarnate, which our bodies have born. The otherwise—in manifold ways, some tiny, some magnificent, many discordant with one another—has always, thanks be, persisted. Dark and queer holiness persists. It needs no invention.

Jewish theologian Melissa Raphael interrupted a patriarchal tendency to read theology in the Holocaust as one of absence. She demarcated care, even in its most infinitesimal and desperate gestures, as holy presence. She insisted

99   James Cone, *The Cross and the Lynching Tree* (Maryknoll, NY: Orbis, 2011).
100  Althaus-Reid, *Indecent Theology*.
101  Alexis Pauline Gumbs, *Dub: Finding Ceremony* (Durham, NC: Duke University Press, 2020).

that relational tenderness evidences holy tenacity even when hegemonic definitions of godlike action fail to detect it.[102]

So too with today's sacramental possibilities otherwise. They are not missing from the present moment. They may have been so scorned or villainized that you cannot recognize them. Or, though your dreams are full of otherwise spaces, your access to them may be impeded by any number of oppressive structures. Or, you may—even now—be reading these words well seated in the folds of such an otherwise. The otherwise persists.

And the otherwise insists into the future, moves toward new incarnation.[103] As Monica Coleman might say, it is making a way out of no way, all the time.[104] Thus in this other sense, the otherwise *always* needs invention. It does not remain inflated by itself. It is between us; it is an active, tactile between-of-us. It expands like the space between sides of the lung; it empties and reopens again elsewhere.

The otherwise needs persistent reinvention in this sense: the otherwise is not some cave that exists out there somewhere, sturdy and trustworthy, which we can find and in which we can take refuge from empire. Empire has left us no pure spaces on this planet. The otherwise is instead a cavern we become together; we are the geodes lining its crevice. Our "we" here exceeds the categories of "man" or

---

102   Melissa Raphael, *The Female Face of God in Auschwitz: A Jewish Feminist Theology of the Holocaust* (London: Routledge, 2003).

103   Catherine Keller writes of the insisting presence of the lure of the divine. The whole framework of process thought gives another framework for imagining otherwise possibility. See her *On the Mystery: Discerning God in Process* (Minneapolis: Fortress, 2007); and Monica Coleman, *Making a Way Out of No Way: A Womanist Theology* (Minneapolis: Fortress, 2008).

104   Coleman, *Making a Way*.

human, exceeding the categories of what Christomodernity has classified as life. This is the space of animal, of ancestry, of colonized other. This is the ugly dark queer otherwise of imperial death. And it is a sparklingly beautiful crystal cave: a stalagmite cathedral of persistent life. Here we breathe life between us.

And the chrism of the colonized other Jesus of Nazareth fits here too. Some geodes are wet with it; the cave is damp with the particular potency that Christian sacrament offers. Nonmodern crevices in fields of imperial power do not depend on Christians to carve their ephemeral breathing spaces, but there is a wet fecundity, a chrism for the otherwise, that Christians bear and embody for this earth. It is a calling: Christians, assemble otherwise. Interrupt, innovate, improvise. Spill your chrism in the relational interstices marked heathen by imperial death systems. Spill your chrism in the coalitional crevices marked sinful even by the death systems of your own church. Such is the great commission.

Your chrism is not the only holy fecundity available in the otherwise. But it is potent, vital, beautiful: offer it to the geology of tomorrow, though the eschatology of such an improvisational ecclesiology remains unrevealed.

The chrism you bear into the interstices of a wounded world is a chrism itself already composed of difference. We bear Christ as chrism into coalitions across difference, crevices of otherwise, where we can together feed and feel and heal, but the chrism itself is also structured across difference. Its molecules are similar caverns, microscopic metaphors: on close inspection, we find that the chrism comprises a bit of sea water from Miriam's hand, sprayed off in jubilation as she sang of liberation; a crumb the Syrophoenician woman claimed from under the men's table; and a trace of sand buried beside the Canaanite's goddess figure as tradition sought to erase her.

Chrism was always a coalitional tenacity across discordant encounters, woven over the stories and contexts into a roughly syncopated continuity around the repetition of a God's claim to be with a people regardless.

Christian chrism, a fluid Christ, is like a suspended solution of holy meeting across difference. There is the fragile possibility, then, that consensually anointing otherwise spaces with our chrism—by being in the assemblies there, by embodying sacrament in these coalitional lungs of the future—might strengthen our communal capacity for holding open the otherwise, because our chrism can be a lubrication of that same microstructure. There are no guarantees with the resistance to empire, but chrism spilled for the world can be a gift for the otherwise in this way. Chrism, fluid Christ, marks defamed bodies as sacred and leaves a glowing trail of ongoing incarnation.

Christian chrism, the concrete stuff of baptism and healing, is not some substance Jesus carried around in his robe; the chrism is elemental to Christ's own body, a fluid body. Christ (*christos*) is anointing, is a messianic moisture that lends itself to the healing and mending of worlds. Sometimes we know how to recognize and convey it in baptismal oil and water, or in bread and wine in the Eucharist. The molecules of these sacred elements are microcosmic structures of otherwise difference, and with them we might strengthen or magnify or beautify the otherwise spaces in which we assemble, which we help carve out.

So, complicit church, in your circulations of Christo-modern power, assemble otherwise: Christian sacrament *is* otherwise.

## Theologizing Otherwise

There will be no corpus or canon for whatever theologizing we will be doing to untangle from power over/through. It will theologize in a spontaneity and sometimes ephemerality that is necessarily diasporic and emergent, often montage.[105] Its words will be too slippery for creeds. In an echo of Pentecost, no one iteration will speak to all hearers. Various iterations, equally truthful, will be discordant.

You won't know for sure that you are in the midst of this theologizing, as its speaker or its audience. It will be ever provisional with no purity test (such a test being a master's tool). It will unfurl like the frond of a fern, fanning your beloved for a day, or tickling your skin in a seductive way, or giving an old woman a pattern of shadow to trace, or inviting the play of a child or your cat.

You can't preserve it and pass it on to another generation. What you pass on instead is the passion or thirst for this way of living, a passion for Christian practice, as a witness to life itself, to holy potential, to healing emergence from

---

105   See Mark D. Jordan, "In Search of Queer Theology Lost," in *Sexual Disorientations: Queer Temporalities, Affects, Theologies*, ed. Kent L. Brintall, Joseph A. Marchal, and Stephen D. Moore (New York: Fordham University Press, 2018), particularly 300–301.

every angle—land, air, womb, sweat, sky—and those all respirate what the masters have tried to control and contain as "God." To do this queer theologizing is to breathe onto and with one another. We conspire. A kiss, a laugh, a grand release (it's queer, after all).

Kerygma in this context helps breath go deeper into our diaphragms. It helps life flow in our differently formed bodies from whatever is our root to whatever is our crown. It opens us to God emerging in all dimensions of our life together. It does not put us to sleep or numb us to feeling, promising reward in death.

Queer theologizing vivifies particular diffuse discordant revelations of self—your self, our selves, God's own self—a biodiversity of the godhead, plural God biomes, not all of which will survive as they vie for space and attention. This provisional theologizing provides an enduring splendor to trust anyhow: as sure as another rain—or as sure as decomposition, bacteria, or the burning of distant stars—and the rotation of cosmic gravities we do not comprehend but in which we flow. We emerge again and again in the power of a holy kinetics, dancing and reveling and struggling it in, the cosmic milk of the multiverse, our God, our holy, our communion.

Can you imagine, churches, that we've been so wrapped in the death-dealing business of modern mechanics, policing bioboxes of colonial dichotomy, that we may have missed *that*? But you may have noticed how numb you feel, how hard it is to feel, or how off things feel when you feel at all.

Yet the hope of ancestors and the Spirit that stirred at creation is still near at hand, and divesting of church as you have known it will not mean an abandonment by our God. A thousand biblical verses assure you of this. The Bible is not biopower, though it is continually deployed as a master's tool. Its old, loose words and discordant revelations can cozy up with the ferns, inviting you to a picnic of midrash.

The theologizing I am describing here cannot be circumscribed by the word "Christianity"—it may well happen outside Christian practice, and that is part of the point and necessity. As we've seen, Christianity has itself been a driving force of modern coloniality and the embedded programming of biopower that makes an obscured distortion of Christianity as intimate as the plastics in our tissues. So inured to this contamination, it is needful to relax the boundary patrols of what is Christian and what is not in order to feel again just how generative and free the flow of holy chrism is.

Theologizing otherwise is not exclusively a Christian possibility, and yet there is unique form to Christian practice. Christian practice does persist with distinct contours apart from biopower, and it is our calling as Christians to be about this practice.[106] Christian practice engages emergent power for others and the earth: lending holy power out and over, giving it away, boosting it out to satisfy need. Christian practice generates power by creatively sharing, diffusing, and offering it, for purposes beyond our own and sometimes beyond its name. Doing so can iterate ongoing incarnation

---

106  I have written elsewhere of practicing chrism (see my article "Christ as Chrism, Christ Given Away"), or I have written, at more length, of kenotic practice (see my book *Power For*).

of Christ's sweat and blood; doing so resurrects our own new subjectivities because Christ midwives our becoming.[107]

Even this posture, a posture I describe as kenotic or christic, is not "ours" to own. It emerges elsewhere too, thank goodness. It is, however, our charism. Our drippy task and joy with which we anoint this earth and, consensually, other bodies. It glistens, draws attention to the holy; it widens the capacities for more emergence and complexity for life. That this has been given into our hands is no small thing; that donation is cause for awe. This is my body, given for you, do this for remembrance of me. Drink of it, all of you, this is my blood, shed for you and for all people, do this in remembrance of me.

Althaus-Reid shows us that these systems and symbols limit *God*. It's not just a (massive) problem for human flourishing; it limits God's own flourishing. God needs queer lovers to lure God out of the closet. God needs the rosary beads wet with your sweat and fragranced by the incense of sex at the dance club, in the alley, and on your bed.

Osagyefo Uhuru Sekou writes that "by highlighting the excesses of the empire and the emptiness of the church, one is cast out of the traditional institutions and intuitions, but this is a gift."[108] And Butler writes that through embodiments of impossible fantasy, we bring the elsewhere home.[109] We

---

107  I have written of Christ as doula or midwife in my chapter, "Christ and the Imperative of Subjectivity," in *Transformative Lutheran Theologies: Feminist, Womanist, and Mujerista Perspectives*, ed. Mary J. Streufert (Minneapolis: Fortress, 2010).

108  Osagyefo Uhuru Sekou, *Gods, Gays, and Guns: Religion and Future of Democracy* (St. Louis, MO: Chalice, 2017), 14.

109  Butler, *Undoing Gender*, 29.

are cast out; we are coalescing new precarious and beautiful homes. For the body. As sacrament.

Queer theologizing functions as a liberatory (and libertine) scene, "which allows us to search for the Queer who is entombed in us, pointing us to a different praxis of the holy in our lives."[110] Coalitional embodiments of divine presence as and with Black, brown, and queer joy and power widen the fissures in modernity's suffocating categories and bring the elsewhere home.

God's spirit becomes anemic on the "light" side of the colonial/modern gender system, moving through a circulatory weakness of white man / white woman / reproduction. Yet the Spirit harkens to the cries of Hagar's baby and the blood of Abel screaming up from the earth; God's spirit haunts these places, ready for embodiment in queer love and Black joy.

God's spirit comes into embodiment in creaturely, dark fecundity and joy and lust. (And this may sound offensive and heretical because it is so thoroughly marked indecent in a Christomodern frame.) God was always there in creaturely dark fecundity, from the *ruach* amid *tohu va-vohu* to the regurgitating innards of Jonah's whale to the womb of an unwed young Galilean under empire. If we have trouble recognizing this God, it is not because God is in actuality the more familiar colonizer deity, shining in light, but because we are yet to embody and live into the shape of our God, which is also to live into the great creaturely potential stirring in our flesh, luring us into a fantastical tomorrow, for and with the

---

110    Althaus-Reid, *Queer God*, 154.

holy, which we cannot yet depict but which we brush against in both gay pride and gay shame,[111] in womxn's pleasured sweat, and in Black and brown joy.

Alexis Pauline Gumbs speaks of an ancestor finding breath again after the suffocating enslavement of the ship's hold, and how "in that moment she knew that whatever made her capable of making breath was not specific enough to be lost."[112] Coming out of the confines of Christomodernity's strongholds, still in the times of its power—may survivors pull breath into their lungs, may they together be lungs of otherwise breath, their inhale opening space otherwise, as holiness spills tenaciously forward.

---

111   David M. Halperin and Valerie Traub, eds., *Gay Shame* (Chicago: University of Chicago Press, 2009).

112   Gumbs, *Dub*, 43.

# Afterword

I t was the mid-'90s. I was a teen and already passionate for church ministry in a way that made my friends roll their eyes affectionately. Meanwhile, "sexual misconduct" cases were tearing up the churches I already loved. My bishop resigned due to a long-ago affair, and one of my pastors had to leave after dating someone in the congregation. Off at college, my campus minister was forced by her diocese to resign because she was out as lesbian, and I remember the shared sense of bereavement in our group at having her taken from us.

At college, I was studying conflict resolution in preparation for going to seminary; I knew at the time that I wanted to work with churches in conflict. At the time, it just seemed coincidental that all the conflicts in my churches happened to be around sexuality. I didn't stop to wonder at the prevalence of sexuality as the focal nexus of all these conflicts. It wasn't until years later, having studied feminist and womanist theology and gender studies, that I looked backward and realized the common theme of those church struggles witnessed in my adolescence.

As we've explored here, it is not simply that the church is prone to fights about sexuality. Through my studies between fields, teaching gender studies one day and theology the next, I've slowly taken myself down a conceptual mine shaft, way down into the tangle, without really realizing what I was searching out, and have found buried deep the evidence of ways that the church built the thing with which it is now contaminated, the ways the church has fashioned the plastic now poisoning its cognition and spiritual awareness. I write yelling up from the angle of this buried awareness, flashlight on the smudged signature at the edge of my map.

And from this vantage, it seems that, even for my most sympathetic church colleagues, it will never be enough, our proclaiming that God loves everyone regardless of their sexuality, our telling of God's biggest embrace. It will not be enough to preach expansive divine love from within conceptual and juridical structures that contradict that love.

It's not enough because we must divest our churches from the poisonous mechanics we have fashioned in order to flow more fluidly as Christian body with the circulating love God has always been pouring out. As a Christomodern church locked in a posture, as Luther would say, *incurvatus in se ipsum*, or we are curled in upon ourselves. We respond ad nauseum to the fallouts of the sexuality we have constructed, and even at our most loving, we perpetrate the toxic construction. Finally, we are now suffocating as a church; it is becoming hard to do church without sexuality—we cannot remember what else we were or what else we do.

We need to divest as Christians from our hold on the sexing and racing mechanics of coloniality and trust that there will still be something left of Christian life apart from this, something worth living for together. Divesting of our hold on power in these debates is a key first step, perhaps the key, to any movement toward healing or new generativity as human bodies in Christian assemblage. Whom we touch or enjoy in bed, how or if we marry, if or with whom we birth—all of these things need to matter (materially, economically, emotionally) far less as core Christian markers if we as a church are to let go of our terror grip on this concept of sexuality in favor of returning our attention to whatever the gospel can mean for us.

This does not mean we stop talking about injustice and pain in our world, or about justice and flourishing, or about any of the material and spiritual realities of things like caressing or partnering or birthing. I imagine and hope that the gospel will keep calling us there. But we will resist falling through the trapdoors in those topics down tunnels of "sexuality," which will again focus on supposedly private or core matters and pull us away from our complicity in creating the conditions we are discussing and will make us again comfortable in the bad patterns of our colonial past as churches.

I think, for example, of clergy sexual abuse. We should not stop addressing this directly. Clergy persons producing harm and hurt must be stopped. Victim-survivors need priority. We can analyze and work to stop harm and support healing and repair without waving banners of sexuality and sexual deviance. For those banners will distract us into the inner desires of the abuser and the inner harms done to the abused, and we will not think widely enough about either the ways the entire clergy structure holds up sexual norms or the ways in which all survivors are more than the sexualized wounds we bear and are often extremely generative collaborators in resistance.

I think also of "homosexuality" as the central topic that has divided many churches in my lifetime. We become so caught up in deciding what is or is not permissible in these sexual categories that we have created with ever-finer scrutiny. Those churches that have moved toward greater inclusion for LGBTQIA members have largely done so by making them more "normal," more like the straight church families we know (often involving the elision of *B* and *I* and any identities harder to press into binaries).[1] Whole groups of people leave and form new churches if their denomination decides that a gay pastor could lead the church. Indeed, as Cocks and Houlbrook write, "Sex would, in the twentieth century, be named, discussed and regulated as never before."[2] While we sit in church councils deliberating just how gay you can be and still pastor or marry or be part of the church (e.g., my own denomination affirms gay clergy but expects them to conform to a covenantal relationship, an affirmation that reinstates a heterosexist, racist marriage structure), we are doing the work of Christian biopower, no matter which side of the debate we come down on. Whether we will say that Christian churches are for man-and-woman families or whether we will say that queer families are welcome in the church, we are doing our maintenance work as a biopower structure in modern society.

---

1   See Marcus C. Tye, "Bye-Bye Bi? Bailey, Biphobia, and Girlie-Men," in *Men Speak Out: Views on Gender, Sex, and Power*, 2nd ed., ed. Shira Tarrant, 87–93 (Hoboken, NJ: Taylor and Francis, 2013); and B. K. Hipsher, "God Is a Many Gendered Thing: An Apophatic Journey to Pastoral Diversity," in *Trans/Formations*, ed. Lisa Isherwood and Marcella Althaus-Reid, Controversies in Contextual Theology, 92–104 (London: SCM, 2009).

2   Cocks and Houlbrook, *Modern History of Sexuality*, 9.

Is this the role of the churches? Is this where the work of the gospel is most urgently needed in your community or in the world today? Whose interests are served by this priority? What needs are not being met in the world while the church keeps its circuits busy maintaining sexuality? And where our maintenance of sexuality is tending the vulnerable (as with abuse of children, for example), are there other ways to serve these same vulnerable persons without recourse to "sexuality"?

As we've seen, "sexuality" is worth avoiding as a disciplinary structure that enacts its own forms of abuse and violence, even violence toward the self, but its traction in modern thought is deep. Interrupting its terms of judgment in ourselves, terms that are so very normal, is hard work. "Your sexuality" likely feels like yours—and race and gender likely figure largely as categories in your life too. This is how many (not all) of us have been taught to think, and indeed how we have been taught to be bodies. This is a lot to interrupt. Incarnation otherwise begins to feel beyond conception.

Admittedly, it can be hard to go through your day with the mantra "colonial/modern gender system" on your tongue in order to decode the pernicious habits of the normal! For a while, just try to pull any loose thread around sexuality that crosses your awareness to discover what can unravel. When you are feeling or thinking about your own sexual thought or practices in terms of your sexual identity, note that thread. If you are leading a premarital counseling session to prepare for a couple's wedding at your church, notice how assumptions of "sexuality" are informing the

conversation, even tacitly. Note the dynamics if you are trying to offer guidance or teaching to youth about sex and
assuming they have nascent sexualities inside them. Note it
when you see a news story about sexual violence or even
hate crimes based on gender identity or sexuality, and you
feel your mind and body making sense of it by putting the
new information into the same old categories. Note how
much of your own sense of religious practice is bound up in
notions of sexual conduct, such that faith practice equates to
sexual practice.

Unravel a regime in your thinking and more deeply,
over time, in your embodiment, and in our embodiments as
Christian assembly. This is a decolonizing process.

Can we still talk about things we have compartmental-
ized into "sexuality" during this decolonization? Yes. We
still have bodies, and in decolonization, we settle more affir-
matively into them. We can talk about pleasure, talk about
bodies, talk about love, talk about Christ. As montage, as
provisional art.

What difference does it make to recognize Christianity's
obsessions with sex as a case of our having fallen into our
own trap? After all, we still have concrete lives to live and
decisions that we have called "sexual" to make. The difference is that it foregrounds the question, What else can
Christian assembly be or do? That is, What have Christians
neglected when preoccupied as church with "sexuality?"
What else can christic embodiment offer? This also offers
Christians the opportunity to practice a different relationship to power, more sustaining and more generative, more

widely shared. To actively practice decolonizing our bodies as a Christian practice.

This gets us to the next difference it makes: it helps us realize that Christians are quite often still doing or supporting harm through their teachings about sexuality. And third, it helps us return to our own life decisions with the weight now shifted off of questions of "sexuality" and onto questions of Christian life (because they are not, after all, the same thing) and then approach the "sexual" aspects of bodily life (the aspects of bodies, friendships, pleasure, and erotics that persist when the bigger apparatus of "sexuality" is dropped) within that wider framework of Christian life. Which is to say, discipleship, or faithfulness, free of the confining cultural mechanisms with which we have preoccupied ourselves as church for far too long, doing far too much harm. Gender, "sexuality," violence, church: too familiar a litany. Time to be on with the work of the Christian assembly, embodied otherwise.

Foucault writes that a great irony is that we have come to see in the discourses of sexuality a mode of liberation, when in fact, as he has argued, the discourses of sexuality are modes of social control. While the gay liberation movement would hold on to "sexuality" and sexual "identity" as touchstones of justification for liberation, Foucault saw that those very concepts were part of a widespread system that inhibits freedom.

Foucault's point speaks to today's churches. Especially for the progressive churches, it can seem that in addressing concerns around sexuality and in articulating welcoming stances on them, we are opening a path of liberation. Certainly, on some concrete levels, we are, just as LGBTQIA activist movements have in many places created significantly more open societies, with concrete legal protections. But as I have argued here, we are still tending the project of sexuality, still devoting our energy into its maintenance, even when it feels like a good cause, and it can be true of progressive church communities addressing sexuality that "the irony of this deployment is in having us believe that our 'liberation' is in the balance," as Foucault writes in the last sentence of his first volume on sexuality.[3]

In some ways, my dispatch is a strange location for working with social theory critiquing Christian political power because this book is itself Christian confession. It is not an outside diagnosis of what is going on with Christian discourse and biopower. Yet bodies confess, and bodies write, not decapitated fields of thought. As confession, this dispatch is itself a resistance against the terms of what confessing Christian subjectivity should be. And when we confess against biopower—which is also to say, against components of our own previous embodied composition—it is never going to be a new discourse writ large, a new canon or faux pacifying orthodoxy. It is provisional and temporary, an interruption that at best stirs others. We confess in the tense interstices of colonial difference, and thus face-to-face, unraveling the governmentality of the pastorate.

Thus this dispatch theologizes while recognizing that theology as such cannot do the work intended here. Theology

---

3  Michel Foucault, *The History of Sexuality*, vol. 1, *An Introduction* (London: Allen Lane, 1979), 159.

as discipline cannot travel into the tension of the colonial difference, but sacred words and holiness can and are already there in any case. This theologizing is in my one voice while recognizing that it cannot resist coloniality unless it becomes a conversation we share, face-to-face or at least word-to-word. I offer words to interrupt, where they can, the grind of Christomodern body commerce. May they interrupt by stirring you to your own words, even to contest what I have written here. Plural we will be. Plural we will be other than the stifled binaries joined in whitewashed oneness that the church would have made of us.

# Selected Bibliography

Ahmed, Sara. *Queer Phenomenology: Orientations, Objects, Others*. Durham, NC: Duke University Press, 2006.

Althaus-Reid, Marcella. *From Feminist Theology to Indecent Theology: Readings on Poverty, Sexual Identity and God*. London: SCM, 2004.

———. "From Liberation Theology to Indecent Theology: The Trouble with Normality in Theology." In *Latin American Liberation Theology: The Next Generation*, edited by Ivan Petrella, 20-38. Maryknoll, NY: Orbis, 2005.

———. *Indecent Theology: Theological Perversions in Sex, Gender, and Politics*. London: Routledge, 2000.

———. *The Queer God*. London: Routledge, 2003.

Bantum, Brian. *The Death of Race: Building a New Christianity in a Racial World*. Minneapolis: Fortress, 2016.

Barreto, Raimundo, and Roberto Sirvent. *Decolonial Christianities: Latinx and Latin American Perspectives*. Cham, Switzerland: Palgrave Macmillan, 2019.

Blencowe, Claire. "Foucault's and Arendt's 'Insider View' of Biopolitics: A Critique of Agamben." *History of the Human Sciences* 23, no. 5 (2010): 113–130.

Bolz-Weber, Nadia. *Shameless: A Sexual Reformation*. New York: Convergent, 2019.

Boyarin, Daniel, and Elizabeth A. Castelli. "Foucault's *The History of Sexuality*: The Fourth Volume, or, A Field Left Fallow for

Others to Till." *Journal of the History of Sexuality* 10, nos. 3/4 (July/October 2001): 357–374.

Brintall, Kent L., Joseph A. Marchal, and Stephen D. Moore, eds. *Sexual Disorientations: Queer Temporalities, Affects, Theologies.* New York: Fordham University Press, 2018.

brown, adrienne maree. *Emergent Strategy: Shaping Change, Changing Worlds.* Chico, CA: AK, 2017.

———. *Pleasure Activism: The Politics of Feeling Good.* Chico, CA: AK, 2019.

Burrus, Virginia. *Chastity as Autonomy: Women in the Stories of the Apocryphal Acts.* Lewiston, NY: Edwin Mellen, 1987.

———. *The Sex Lives of Saints: An Erotics of Ancient Hagiography.* Philadelphia: University of Pennsylvania Press, 2007.

Butler, Judith. *Notes toward a Performative Theory of Assembly.* Cambridge, MA: Harvard University Press, 2015.

———. *Undoing Gender.* New York: Routledge, 2004.

Butler, Judith, and Athena Athanasiou. *Dispossession: The Performative in the Political.* Cambridge: Polity, 2013.

Butler, Judith, Zeynep Gambetti, and Leticia Sabsay, eds. *Vulnerability in Resistance.* Durham, NC: Duke University Press, 2016.

Carter, J. Kameron. "Black Malpractice (or, the Fugitive Sacred)." In *Otherwise Worlds: Against Settler Colonialism and Anti-Blackness,* edited by Tiffany Lethabo King, Jenell Navarro, and Andrea Smith, 158–212. Durham, NC: Duke University Press, 2020.

———. "The Inglorious: With and Beyond Giorgio Agamben." *Political Theology* 14, no. 1 (2013): 77–87.

———. "Paratheological Blackness." *South Atlantic Quarterly* 112, no. 4 (2013): 589–611.

—————. *Race: A Theological Account*. Oxford: Oxford University Press, 2008.

Carter, J. Kameron, and Sarah Jane Cervenak. "Black Ether." *New Centennial Review* 16, no. 2 (Fall 2016): 203–244.

Carvalhaes, Cláudio. *Eucharist and Globalization: Redrawing the Borders of Eucharistic Hospitality*. Eugene, OR: Pickwick, 2013.

—————. *Liturgies from Below: Praying with People at the Ends of the Earth*. Nashville: Abingdon, 2020.

—————. *Praying with Every Heart: Orienting Our Lives to the Wholeness of the World*. Eugene, OR: Cascade, 2021.

Cervenak, Sarah Jane. *Wandering: Philosophical Performances of Racial and Sexual Freedom*. Durham, NC: Duke University Press, 2014.

Chitty, Christopher. *Sexual Hegemony: Statecraft, Sodomy, and Capital in the Rise of the World System*. Durham, NC: Duke University Press, 2020.

Cocks, H. G., and Matt Houlbrook. *The Modern History of Sexuality*. Hampshire, UK: Palgrave Macmillan, 2006.

Crawley, Ashon T. "Held in the Vestibule." *Modern Believing* 60, no. 1 (2019): 49–63.

—————. *The Lonely Letters*. Durham, NC: Duke University Press, 2020.

—————. "Stayed / Freedom / Hallelujah." In *Otherwise Worlds: Against Settler Colonialism and Anti-Blackness*, edited by Tiffany Lethabo King, Jenell Navarro, and Andrea Smith, 27–37. Durham, NC: Duke University Press, 2020.

—————. "Susceptibility." *GLQ* 27, no. 1 (2021): 11–38.

Curtice, Kaitlin B. *Native: Identity, Belonging, and Rediscovering God*. Grand Rapids, MI: Brazos, 2020.

De La Torre, Miguel A. *Burying White Privilege: Resurrecting a Badass Christianity*. Grand Rapids, MI: W. B. Eerdmans, 2019.

DiPietro, Pedro, Jennifer McWeeny, and Shireen Roshanravan, eds. *Speaking Face to Face: The Visionary Philosophy of María Lugones*. Albany: State University of New York Press, 2019.

Douglas, Kelly Brown. *Stand Your Ground: Black Bodies and the Justice of God*. Maryknoll, NY: Orbis, 2015.

Draper, Andrew T. *A Theology of Race and Place: Liberation and Reconciliation in the Works of Jennings and Carter*. Eugene, OR: Pickwick, 2016.

Duncan, Lenny. *Dear Church: A Love Letter from a Black Preacher to the Whitest Denomination in the U.S.* Minneapolis: Fortress, 2019.

Evol, Keno. "Daunte Wright: A Billion Clusters of Rebellion and Starlight." Mn Artists: Arts Writing from Mn, Beyond Mn. April 19, 2021. https://mnartists.walkerart.org/daunte-wright-a-billion-clusters-of-rebellion-and-starlight.

———. "Poly-fugitivity: Utopian Relations in Dystopian Structures." Mn Artists: Arts Writing from Mn, Beyond Mn. January 15, 2021. https://mnartists.walkerart.org/poly-fugitivity-utopian-relations-in-dystopian-structures.

Fausto-Sterling, Anne. *Sexing the Body: Gender Politics and the Construction of Sexuality*. New York: Basic Books, 2000.

Foucault, Michel. "The Analytic Philosophy of Politics." *Foucault Studies* 24 ( June 2018): 188–200. Originally 1978, conference paper delivered in Tokyo.

———. *Confessions of the Flesh: The History of Sexuality*. Vol 4. Edited by Frédéric Gros. New York: Pantheon, 2021.

———. *The History of Sexuality Volume 1: An Introduction*. London: Allen Lane, 1978.

Freccero, Carla. *Queer/Early/Modern*. Durham, NC: Duke University Press, 2006.

Freeman, Elizabeth. *Time Binds: Queer Temporalities, Queer Histories*. Durham, NC: Duke University Press, 2010.

Goldman, Danielle. *I Want to Be Ready: Improvised Dance as a Practice of Freedom*. Ann Arbor: University of Michigan Press, 2010.

Gumbs, Alexis Pauline. *Dub: Finding Ceremony*. Durham, NC: Duke University Press, 2020.

———. Foreword to *Beyond Survival: Strategies and Stories from the Transformative Justice Movement*, edited by Ejeris Dixon and Leah Lakshmi Piepzna-Samarasinha, 1–3. Chico, CA: AK, 2020.

Halperin, David M. *Saint Foucault: Towards a Gay Historiography*. Oxford: Oxford University Press, 1995.

Halperin, David M., and Trevor Hoppe, eds. *The War on Sex*. Durham, NC: Duke University Press, 2017.

Halperin, David M., and Valerie Traub, eds. *Gay Shame*. Chicago: University of Chicago Press, 2009.

Halperin, David M., John J. Winkler, and Froma I. Zeitlin, eds. *Before Sexuality: The Construction of Erotic Experience in the Ancient Greek World*. Princeton, NJ: Princeton University Press, 1990.

Hardt, Michael, and Antonio Negri. *Assembly*. Oxford: Oxford University Press, 2017.

———. *Commonwealth*. Cambridge, MA: Belknap Press of Harvard University Press, 2009.

———. *Multitude: War and Democracy in the Age of Empire*. New York: Penguin, 2004.

Hartman, Saidiya. "Venus in Two Acts." *Small Axe* 26, no. 12.2 (June 2008): 1–14.

———. *Wayward Lives, Beautiful Experiments: Intimate Histories of Riotous Black Girls, Troublesome Women, and Queer Radicals*. New York: Norton, 2019.

Haskaj, Fatmir. "From Biopower to Necroeconomies: Neoliberalism, Biopower and Death Economies." *Philosophy and Social Criticism* 44, no. 10 (2018): 1148–1168.

Havea, Jione, ed. *Vulnerability and Resilience: Body and Liberating Theologies*. Minneapolis: Fortress, 2020.

Henderson-Espinoza, Robyn. *Activist Theology*. Minneapolis: Fortress, 2019.

———. "Perversion, Ethics, and Creative Disregard: Indecency as the Virtue to Ethical Perversion." In *Indecent Theologians: Marcella Althaus-Reid and the Next Generation of Postcolonial Activists*, edited by Nicolas Panotto, 213–240. Alameda, CA: Borderless, 2016.

Isherwood, Lisa, and Marcella Althaus-Reid. *Trans/Formations*. Controversies in Contextual Theology. London: SCM, 2009.

Isherwood, Lisa, and Mark D. Jordan, eds. *Dancing Theology in Fetish Boots: Essays in Honor of Marcella Althaus-Reid*. London: SCM, 2010.

Jennings, Willie J. *The Christian Imagination: Theology and the Origins of Race*. New Haven, CT: Yale University Press, 2010.

Jones, Robert P. *White Too Long: The Legacy of White Supremacy in American Christianity*. New York: Simon & Schuster, 2020.

Jordan, Mark D. *Convulsing Bodies: Religion and Resistance in Foucault*. Stanford, CA: Stanford University Press, 2015.

———. *The Ethics of Sex*. Oxford: Blackwell, 2002.

———. "Notes on Camp Theology." In *Dancing Theology in Fetish Boots*, edited by Lisa Isherwood and Mark D. Jordan, 181–190. London: SCM, 2010.

———. "The Return of Religion during the Reign of Sexuality." In *Feminism, Sexuality, and the Return of Religion*, edited by Linda Martín Alcoff and John D. Caputo, 39–54. Bloomington: Indiana University Press, 2011.

Kaba, Mariame. *We Do This 'Til We Free Us: Abolitionist Organizing and Transforming Justice*. Chicago: Haymarket, 2021.

Kamitsuka, Margaret, ed. *The Embrace of Eros: Bodies, Desires, and Sexuality in Christianity*. Minneapolis: Fortress, 2010.

King, Tiffany Lethabo, Jenell Navarro, and Andrea Smith. *Otherwise Worlds: Against Settler Colonialism and Anti-Blackness*. Durham, NC: Duke University Press, 2020.

Lowe, Mary Elise. "Gay, Lesbian, and Queer Theologies: Origins, Contributions, and Challenges." *Dialog: A Journal of Theology* 48, no. 1 (Spring 2009): 49–61.

Lugones, María. "Heterosexualism and the Colonial/Modern Gender System." *Hypatia* 22, no. 1 (Winter 2007): 186–209. https://www.jstor.org/stable/4640051.

———. "On Complex Communication." *Hypatia* 21, no. 3 (Summer 2006): 75–85. https://www.jstor.org/stable/40928654.

———. *Pilgrimages/Peregrinajes: Theorizing Coalition against Multiple Oppressions*. Lanham, MD: Rowman & Littlefield, 2003.

———. "Toward a Decolonial Feminism." *Hypatia* 25, no. 4 (Fall 2010): 742–759. https://www.jstor.org/stable/40928654.

Maier, Harry O. "Soja's Thirdspace, Foucault's Heterotopia and de Certeau's Practice: Time-Space and Social Geography in Emergent Christianity." *Historical Social Research* 38, no. 3 (2013): 76–92.

Marchal, Joseph A. "'Making History' Queerly: Touches across Time through a Biblical Behind." *Biblical Interpretation* 19, no. 4/5 (April 2011): 373–395.

Martin, Dale B. "Familiar Idolatry and the Christian Case against Marriage." In *Sexuality and the Sacred: Sources for Theological Reflection*, 2nd ed., edited by Marvin M. Ellison and Kelly Brown Douglas, 412–436. Louisville, KY: Westminster John Knox, 2010.

Martin, Luther H., Huck Gutman, and Patrick H. Hutton. *Technologies of the Self: A Seminar with Michel Foucault.* Amherst: University of Massachusetts Press, 1988.

Mbembe, Achille. *Necropolitics.* Translated by Steve Corcoran. Durham, NC: Duke University Press, 2019.

———. *Out of the Dark Night: Essays on Decolonization.* New York: Columbia University Press, 2021.

McClintock, Anne. *Imperial Leather: Race, Gender, and Sexuality in the Colonial Contest.* London: Routledge, 1995.

Moore, Stephen D. *God's Beauty Parlor: And Other Queer Spaces in and around the Bible.* Stanford, CA: Stanford University Press, 2001.

Moten, Fred. *In the Break: The Aesthetics of the Black Radical Tradition.* Minneapolis: University of Minnesota Press, 2003.

Moyse, Ashley John. *The Art of Living for a Technological Age: Toward a Humanizing Performance.* Minneapolis: Fortress, 2021.

Panotto, Nicolas, ed. *Indecent Theologians: Marcella Althaus-Reid and the Next Generation of Postcolonial Activists.* Alameda, CA: Borderless, 2016.

Perkinson, James. *White Theology: Outing Supremacy in Modernity.* New York: Palgrave Macmillan, 2004.

Perry, Imani. *Vexy Thing: On Gender and Liberation.* Durham, NC: Duke University Press, 2018.

Ramirez, Erica M. "Race and Global Renewal: Mulattic Tongues and Hybridic Imaginations to the Ends of the Earth." *Pneuma* 36, no. 3 (2014): 379–385.

Raphael, Melissa. *The Female Face of God in Auschwitz: A Jewish Feminist Theology of the Holocaust.* London: Routledge, 2003.

Rieger, Joerg, and Kwok Pui-lan. *Occupy Religion: Theology of the Multitude.* Lanham, MD: Rowman & Littlefield, 2012.

Rivera, Mayra. *Poetics of the Flesh.* Durham, NC: Duke University Press, 2015.

Rubin, Gayle S. "Thinking Sex: Notes for a Radical Theory of the Politics of Sexuality." In *The Lesbian and Gay Studies Reader*, edited by Henry Abelove, Michèle Aina Barale, and David M. Halperin, 3–44. London: Routledge, 1993.

Sands, Kathleen M. "Uses of the Thea(o)logian: Sex and Theodicy in Religious Feminism." *Journal of Feminist Studies in Religion* 8, no. 1 (1992): 7–33.

Schneider, Laurel. "Promiscious Incarnation." In *The Embrace of Eros: Bodies, Desires, and Sexuality in Christianity*, edited by Margaret Kamitsuka, 231–246. Minneapolis: Fortress, 2010.

———. "What Race Is Your Sex?" In *Disrupting White Supremacy from Within: White People on What We Need to Do*, edited by Jennifer Harvey, Karen A. Case, and Robin Hawley Gorsline, 142-62. Cleveland, OH: Pilgrim, 2004.

Sekou, Osagyefo Uhuru. *Gods, Gays, and Guns: Religion and Future of Democracy.* St. Louis, MO: Chalice, 2017.

Sharpe, Christina. "Black Studies: In the Wake." *Black Scholar: Journal of Black Studies and Research* 44, no. 2 (June 2014): 59–69.

———. *In the Wake: On Blackness and Being.* Durham, NC: Duke University Press, 2016.

Spillers, Hortense J. "Mama's Baby, Papa's Maybe: An American Grammar Book." *Diacritics* 17, no. 2 (Summer 1987): 64–81.

Stanley, Eric A., and Nat Smith, eds. *Captive Genders: Trans Embodiment and the Prison Industrial Complex*. Expanded 2nd ed. Oakland, CA: AK, 2015.

Sverker, Joseph. *Human Being and Vulnerability: Beyond Constructivism and Essentialism in Judith Butler, Steven Pinker, and Colin Gunton*. Stuttgart: Ibidem-Verlag, 2020.

Talvacchia, Kathleen T., Mark Larrimore, and Michael F. Pettinger, eds. *Queer Christianities: Lived Religion in Transgressive Forms*. New York: New York University Press, 2014.

Taylor, Charles. *Modern Social Imaginaries*. Durham, NC: Duke University Press, 2004.

———. *A Secular Age*. Cambridge, MA: Belknap Press of Harvard University Press, 2007.

———. *Sources of the Self: The Making of Modern Identity*. Cambridge, MA: Harvard University Press, 1989.

Valenti, Jessica. *The Purity Myth: How America's Obsession with Virginity Is Hurting Young Women*. New York: Seal, 2019.

Viefhues-Bailey, Ludger H. *Between a Man and a Woman? Why Conservatives Oppose Same-Sex Marriage*. New York: Columbia University Press, 2010.

Weheliye, Alexander G. *Habeas Viscus: Racializing Assemblages, Biopolitics, and Black Feminist Theories of the Human*. Durham, NC: Duke University Press, 2014.

West, Traci C. *Solidarity and Defiant Spirituality: Africana Lessons on Religion, Racism, and Ending Gender Violence*. New York: New York University Press, 2019.

Wiesner-Hanks, Merry. *Christianity and Sexuality in the Early Modern World: Regulating Desire, Reforming Practice*. London: Routledge, 2000.

———, ed. *Convents Confront the Reformation: Catholic and Protestant Nuns in Germany*. Milwaukee: Marquette University Press, 1996.